THE ANGELIC WAY

Also by Rami Shapiro

The Sacred Art of Lovingkindness: Preparing to Practice

Ethics of the Sages: Pirke Avot

The Divine Feminine in Biblical Wisdom Literature:
Selections Annotated & Explained

Let Us Break Bread Together: A Passover Haggadah for Christians
(*with Michael Smith*)

Open Secrets: The Letters of Reb Yerachmiel ben Yisrael

The Hebrew Prophets: Selections Annotated & Explained

Hasidic Tales: Annotated & Explained

The Way of Solomon:
Finding Joy and Contentment in the Wisdom of Ecclesiastes

Minyan: Ten Principles for Living a Life of Integrity

THE ANGELIC WAY

Angels through the Ages and Their Meaning for Us

❧

RAMI SHAPIRO

BlueBridge

Cover design by Angel Guerra

Cover art: Sano di Pietro (1406–1481), Angel of the Annunciation, *2nd half
15th cen., Musée du Petit Palais, Avignon, France. Photo credit: Réunion des
Musées Nationaux / Art Resource, NY*

Text design by Cynthia Dunne

Copyright © 2009 by Rami Shapiro

Library of Congress Cataloging-in-Publication Data

Shapiro, Rami M.
The angelic way : angels through the ages and their meaning for us
/ Rami Shapiro.
p. cm.
Includes bibliographical references and index.
ISBN 978-1-933346-19-9
1. Angels. I. Title.
BT966.3.S53 2009
202'.15—dc22
2009021242

Published by
B l u e B r i d g e
An imprint of
United Tribes Media Inc.
240 West 35th Street, Suite 500
New York, NY 10001

www.bluebridgebooks.com

Printed in the United States of America

10 9 8 7 6 5 4 3 2 1

Contents

❧

To Gabriel

On Angels' Wings

ৼৡ৵

WHY DO ANGELS have wings? It may seem like an odd question, but there is no necessity for angels to be winged. It is not as if angels were physical beings who needed wings to provide them with a lift. God could have fashioned them without wings and still endowed them with the capacity for flight. So, why do angels have wings?

The ancient Greek philosopher Plato (ca. 428–348 BCE) provides an answer in his dialogue called *Phaedrus*: "By their nature wings have the power to lift up heavy things and raise them aloft where the gods all dwell, and so, more than anything that pertains to the body, they are akin to the divine, which has beauty, wisdom, goodness, and everything of that sort."[1]

The wings remind us of God. Angels are messengers from God (*angeloi* means messenger in Greek, as does the older Hebrew word for angels, *malak* [singular] and *malakhim* [plural]) and wear their wings as a sign of the divine. The wings are powerful symbols. In *The Angelic Way* we will extend the symbolic from the wing to the entire winged creature: for us angels themselves are symbols, metaphors not only of God reaching out to us, but of us reaching out to God.

Do we then also have to state whether or not God is "real" or, like the angels, a metaphor?

We cannot say anything about God that is *not* metaphoric. This does not in itself imply that God does not exist—such a question is beyond the scope of this book. But it does mean quite clearly that all our talk about God is, to borrow from the Buddhists, "a finger pointing to the moon," and not the moon itself.

In the opening chapter of the *Tao Te Ching* (the eighty-one poems attributed to the sixth-century BCE Chinese sage Lao Tzu that form the foundation of philosophical Taoism) we read, "The Tao that can be named is not the Eternal Tao" (*Tao Te Ching*, 1:1).[2] The name is not the named; the map is not the land; the notes are not the music. Yet we humans forever seem driven to name, as the innumerable gods, goddesses, spirits, and demons across the ages—and all the theological talk associated with them—attest to.

The problem is not the human passion for names, but the human predilection to mistake the name for the named. Here we will do our best not to make that mistake. Let us state up front that we are examining myths, symbols, and metaphors. Yet this does not make ours a lesser venture. Myths, symbols, and metaphors are the ways in which we humans point to ultimate reality.

We imagine angels with wings because angels are metaphoric representations of the human capacity to move between levels of consciousness, opening the least inclusive level of our awareness to the most inclusive level of our awareness, where the whole world is seen as the manifestation of God, the Source and Substance of all reality. As the scholar of religion Peter Berger writes,

> Everything is full of gods, exclaimed Thales of Miletus. Biblical monotheism swept away the gods in the glorification of the majesty of the One, but the fullness that overwhelmed Thales continued to live for a long time in the figures of the angels, those beings of light who are witness of the fullness of the divine glory. In the prophetic visions they surround the throne of God. Again and again, in the pages of the Old and New Testaments, they appear as messengers (*angeloi*) of this God, signalizing His transcendence as well as His presence in the world of man . . . In the religious view of reality, all phenomena point toward that which transcends them, and this transcendence actively impinges from all sides on the empirical sphere of human existence.[3]

Peter Berger's notion that "all phenomena point toward that which transcends them" is crucial to our understanding of angels as symbols of, or metaphors for, the human capacity to transcend our least inclusive level of awareness—our ego-centered mind or consciousness—toward the most inclusive level, which is God-centered spirit or consciousness. Angels are symbolic of the ability of all human beings for self-improvement: this is our angelic capacity or faculty, our angelic potential.

We humans are more than we let on, more than we admit, more than we know. We are bodies, certainly; few if any of us deny that. For some that is all we are—material forms complex enough to generate the effervescence of consciousness. For others we are a bit more: we are bodies and minds, the latter inhabiting the former, but so reliant on it that when the body dies, the mind dies, too.

But many of us believe that we are also, and even primarily, souls—extra-physical entities that lie behind or within the ego-centered mind, a bit like *matryoshka*, Russian nesting dolls: the smaller soul nested in the slightly larger mind, which is itself nested in the even larger body.

In *The Angelic Way*, however, we invert the order, and follow the lead of William Blake, the English mystic, artist, and poet who in the 1790s wrote in his *The Marriage of Heaven and Hell*, "Man has no Body distinct from his Soul for that call'ed Body is a portion of Soul discern'd by the five Senses, the chief inlets of Soul in this age."[4] For Blake there was but one "body," the soul that is both material when looked at through our senses and immaterial when looked at through the imagination.

But to take Blake's insight further, not only are we humans body, mind, and soul—we are also spirit. We are (at least) like a four-part *matryoshka*. Body, in our view, is not the largest doll but the smallest, being surrounded by ego-centered mind, world-centered soul, and God-centered spirit, respectively. The body in and of itself is not self-reflexive; it runs itself but does not know itself. And because it is thus limited, we will have little to say about it in this book. Our focus is on ego-centered mind, world-centered soul, and God-centered spirit, and the role the angelic potential plays in and between each of these three levels or dimensions.

The ego-centered mind is that aspect of ourselves that says "I," "me," and "mine." It sees itself as separate from and alien to the world, and relates to everything and everyone in the world as "other," as objects, a relationship that the twentieth-century Jewish philosopher Martin Buber called *I-It*.

The world-centered soul is that aspect of ourselves that sees us as part of the world rather than apart from it, as equal subjects. Buber called this engaging the world from the perspective of *I-Thou*. Here we recognize that difference is not to be feared but appreciated, and see that all things are alive with purpose, meaning, and intrinsic value. Here we "love our neighbor as our self" because we see that each neighbor is a self equal in value to ourselves.

The God-centered spirit is the largest and most inclusive dimension of human consciousness. Where the ego-centered mind sees self and world as separate, and the world-centered soul sees self and world as part of a single whole, God-centered spirit sees itself as all-inclusive, as *I-I*. God is the ego-centered mind as well as the world-centered soul, *and* that which embraces and transcends them both. The ego-centered mind says to the other, "What are you?" The world-centered soul asks the other, "Who are you?" The God-centered spirit simply tells the other, "I am you!"

These three dimensions of consciousness are not closed to one another. Indeed, since the narrow ego-centered mind and the mutual world-centered soul are both part of the final, nondual God-centered spirit (nondual means that everything is part of the One, like all waves are part of the ocean), there is no gap between these dimensions at all. But they differ in their degree of inclusivity, the way a letter differs from the word in which it rests, and the word differs from the sentence of which it is a part. Given their interrelatedness it is possible for each dimension to connect with the others, and angels are metaphors for this connecting.

Myths of angels descending to earth are metaphors of God-centered spirit entering into ego-centered mind. Myths of angels ascending to heaven, and of humans being transformed into angels, are metaphors of world-centered soul entering into God-centered spirit. And myths of humans rising to heaven and then returning to earth are metaphors of the human capacity to awaken fully to (and not just glimpse) the nondual nature of I-I.

In the Hebrew Bible God-centered spirit speaks of itself as *Ehyeh asher Ehyeh* (Exodus 3:14). While most English Bibles translate the Hebrew as "I am that I am," this static notion of God is the exact opposite of what the Hebrew itself suggests. *Ehyeh* is the future imperfect form of the verb "to be." God—as the author of Exodus wants us to understand God—is not only a matter of being but of becoming. *Ehyeh asher Ehyeh* is better translated as "I will be whatever I will be." Or, to be less precise and perhaps more insightful, "I am becoming whatever is becoming and there is no telling in advance what I will be except to say that whatever is happening I will be that." God is a verb, not a noun; God is the happening of life, the living itself, the birthing, dying, crying, laughing, wild dancing of all reality perpetually surprising itself with its own creativity.

God is not other than the ego-centered mind or the world-centered soul—there is nothing other than God.

The ego-centered mind cannot, in and of itself, come to know itself as the Divine anymore than the acorn can know itself to be the tree. And yet it isn't quite ignorant of this either. We have dreams of something more, visions of something more, myths of something more, and these dreams, visions, and myths often take the form of stories about angels. At the core of this book lies the premise that angels are truly our own angelic potential, enabling the ego-centered mind to articulate its intimations of something greater. Angels are a way for soul and spirit to speak to the mind, and the way the mind comes to make sense of its encounters with soul and spirit. And because our way of meeting angels is through the imaginative faculty of dream, vision, and myth we can say that angels are themselves symbolic creations of the imagination.

Linking the imagination to angels can be traced at least as far back as the ancient Greek philosopher Aristotle (384–322 BCE). In his treatise *De Anima* (On the Soul) Aristotle spoke of active and passive intellects, what we might call "knowing" and "what is known." Knowing is an action, a process, an essentially imaginative faculty by which we move from the known (the passive intellect) to the as yet unknown. From ancient times commentators on Aristotle differed as to whether the active intellect is located inside or outside the human mind. The second-century CE philosopher Alexander of Aphrodisias, the most famous of the ancient Greek commentators on Aristotle, held that the active intellect was external and synonymous with God. Followers of Alexander spoke of the active intellect as an angel, a messenger from God revealing truths to humankind.

The Hebrew word *malak* means both "angel" and "messenger," so the ancient Hebrews and Greeks likely shared the idea that God communicates with humanity through the imaginative faculty of the human mind—that aspect of mind that can open up to what is greater than itself. The angelic messenger is the symbolic link between the human world and the divine world; the angelic way invites us humans to connect with the wider fields of consciousness open to us as world-centered soul and God-centered spirit.

Encounters with angels are often described as meeting actual winged beings—when truly we are meeting greater and more holistic aspects of ourselves. Angels are, in other words, not physical entities but imaginative faculties.

To use a powerful example from the Bible, did an angel literally appear to Moses from within a bush that burned but was not consumed (in Exodus 3:2)? Was the angel "real"? Or is this rather the author's way of telling us that Moses moved from ego-centered mind into the world-centered soul in order to encounter the God-centered spirit—by using his angelic potential?

In this book we interpret Moses's encounter with the angel as a meeting of mind and soul, and then with spirit itself, the one and only "I" who knows itself to be all things. The angelic dimension of humankind, in other words, constitutes the human capacity to experience and integrate ego-centered mind, world-centered soul, and God-centered spirit.

With this premise at the core of *The Angelic Way*, the never-ending human fascination with God's winged messengers is not surprising. The ego-centered mind has a subtle, almost imperceptible intuition of, and longing for, something greater than itself, and angels—our angelic potential—can lift us up to it.

• • •

One star-lit night some three thousand years ago a Hebrew poet—perhaps even King David himself—lay on his back and, gazing into the infinite depths of space, felt dwarfed by the sheer scale of the night sky:

When I peer into Your sky,
The labor of Your fingers,
The moon and the stars that You established:
What is humanity, that You remember them?
And the children of humanity, that You are mindful of them?
You have made humans a little lower than angels,
And crowned them with honor and splendor.
You gave them stewardship over the works of Your hands
And You have set all things at their feet. (Psalm 8:3–6)

For all its recognition of God, this is a first-person poem celebrating the uniqueness of humanity: "When *I* peer into Your sky." No supernatural insight is claimed or offered. The poet, the psalmist, doesn't pretend to know the mind of God, only to question it. The poet in fact does what most of us have done at some point in our lives—looked into the night sky and wondered, who am I?

The question "What is humanity?" is best asked against the background of space's immensity and God's infinity. It is then that all our hubris falls away, and we are left with a pristine and perhaps primordial silence. And what arises for the psalmist from that silence is a bit deeper than the standard English translation lets on.

The psalmist uses the Hebrew *enush*, rightly translated as "humanity." But he does so knowing that his listeners will also hear *ahnush*, "incurable," a word sharing the same spelling as *enush*, differing only in the way the reader or speaker vocalizes the opening letter, *Aleph*. There is something incurable about humankind. We are mortal, and against the black backdrop of the seemingly immortal sky our mortality is all the more poignant.

The psalmist inquires of God, "Why do you bother with these

incurable creatures when the whole universe is Yours to enjoy?" The Hebrew verbs here are *zachar*, "to remember," and *pakad*, meaning both "to be mindful" and "to visit." God not only remembers humanity, God not only considers humanity, God *visits* humanity. Again, with all the worlds glittering above, why does God come to visit this one?

Why does God take an interest in us? Perhaps the answer comes in the next line, "You have made humans a little lower than angels." The Hebrew actually says lower than *elohim*, the "gods," rather than the more standard *malakhim*, "angels." This confusion of God and angels, and the parallel confusion of angels and humans, will be with us throughout this book, and point us toward a deeper, more metaphoric understanding of angels as that capacity of human consciousness that can see all three realms of knowing— ego-centered mind, world-centered soul, and God-centered spirit —as part of a single system of being. Regardless of the psalmist's choice of nouns, however, the question remains: What is it about humankind that matters?

The poet goes on to say that we are crowned with divine glory and given to rule over God's creation, and the reader is left with the notion that this is why God cares. We work for God, and the Lord needs to supervise us now and again to make sure we are following the divine directive. But this is a weak reading of the text.

The poet's observations about humanity's charge to steward nature are not an answer to why God cares, but a further compounding of the original question. Why crown humanity with divine glory? Why give humans dominion over nature when the more lofty angels are better candidates for the task?

The answer is in the original question itself: What draws God to us mortals *is* our incurable mortality. Unlike angels, we humans die. Unlike angels, we humans change. Unlike angels, we humans are unpredictable and hence more interesting, and for these reasons alone worthy of God's attention. God knows in advance what angels are going to do because God created them to do it. God does not know in advance what humans are going to do because God created us with an element of chaos, choice, and free will. What differentiates us from angels and makes us more intriguing to God is our ability for growth. In other words, while angels are a way, who really matters are those who choose to follow the way, or not.

. . .

The human desire to encounter the angelic is universal, regardless of the names given or details told. When a phenomenon is so indigenous to humanity as a whole it is safe to say there is something about angels—and angel-like beings—that is, loosely speaking, woven into our core existence. When we deal with angels we are dealing with archetypal forms of the human intuition of the divine—the "something more" of which we are a part.

Here we are calling that something more "God," and by "God" we mean that nondual reality that manifests as the universe and everything in it. Humanity is a part of God like a wave is part of the ocean, but for most of our existence we are ignorant of this fact. Angels are a means for overcoming that ignorance.

However, we must be clear that when speaking about angels, and about ego-centered mind, world-centered soul, and God-centered spirit, we are speaking metaphorically. And, when we look at the tales of angels and ascended humans who become angels and messengers of God, we are dealing with myth.

If anything said here was taken literally, that is if we began to regard angels as beings separate from ourselves, and ourselves as beings separate from God, then we would miss the core premise of this book. Given the centrality of myth and metaphor in *The Angelic Way*, then, it is necessary to clarify these terms.

When we speak about the deepest levels of human insight and understanding we tend to speak in myth and metaphor. When myths speak of outward journeys, they are really talking about inner ones. When they speak of gods and angels as beings separate from ourselves, they are actually referring to aspects of ourselves. Myth arose at a time in human development when all inner experience was projected outward to make it accessible to human investigation.

Myth is not about outer events but inner ones; not about historical moments but timeless psycho-spiritual processes. While many people may argue to the contrary, *The Angelic Way* is based on the understanding that mythic encounters with angels are *not* records of historical encounters limited to the individuals whose names are associated with them, but rather internal meetings of ego-centered mind with world-centered soul and perhaps even God-centered spirit—all through the capacity of angelic awareness, i.e., that inner human capacity and potential to move from the least inclusive realm of consciousness, the I-It, to the most inclusive realm of consciousness, the I-I.

If we mistake these myths for scientific or historic facts we will likely misunderstand them. This misunderstanding leads some to dismiss myth and the message it carries, while it leads others to dismiss science because it seems to disprove the myth. Both the dismissal and the defense of myth mistake it for something that it isn't—fact.

Joseph Campbell, one of the most influential twentieth-century scholars of comparative religion and mythology, reflected deeply on myth and metaphor. He wrote,

> There is a beautiful saying of Novalis: "The seat of the soul is there, where the outer and the inner worlds meet." That is the wonderland of myth. From the outer world the senses carry images of the mind, which do not become myth, however, until they're transformed by fusion with accordant insights, awakened as imagination from the inner world of the body. The Buddhists speak of Buddha Realms. There are planes and orders of consciousness that can be brought to mind through meditations on appropriately mythologized forms. Plato tells of universal ideas, memory of which is lost at birth but through philosophy may be recalled.[5]

The Greek word *mythus* denotes a story or narrative that, from our perspective, originates in the encounter between ego-centered mind and its angelic capacity for self-transcendence. This is where the I-It yields to the I-Thou, and where the human being begins the journey toward God-centered spirit and the realization that all of creation is a manifestation of the one—God.

In his classic book on myth, *The Hero's Journey*, Joseph Campbell said that "mythology is an organization of symbolic narrative and images that are metaphorical of the possibilities of human experience and fulfillment in a given society at a given time."[6] According to the Campbell scholar Mark Meadows, the function of myth as Campbell understood it is to help the individual realize his or her connection with the Ground of Being—"at once the depths of the psyche and in the transcendent aspect of the macrocosm itself . . . and to thereby see the material world as a symbol of an unseen unity that undergirds and informs the phenomenal world."[7]

Today the term "myth" is often used as a synonym for "false." This is a modernist corruption of its meaning. Myths are not true in the sense that they are factual or historical, they are true in that they reveal in mythopoetic form psycho-spiritual truths about our lives and how best to live them. According to Joseph Campbell, "Like dreams, myths are productions of the human imagination. Their images, consequently—though derived from the material world and its supposed history—are, like dreams, revelations of the deepest hopes, desires and fears, potentialities and conflicts, of the human will—which in turn is moved by the energies of the organs of the body operating variously against each other and in concert. Every myth, that is to say, whether or not by intention, is psychologically symbolic. Its narratives and images are to be read, therefore, not literally, but as metaphors."[8]

Myths are maps in the form of story that have the potential to lead us to the wakening of our most inclusive self. Like all good stories, myths have characters—gods, angels, heroes, heroines, and powers that oppose them—but these are real only in the context of the myth. If we limit ourselves to a superficial reading of myths, their meaning will be lost on us. If, on the other hand, we read myths as maps and see where they lead, we will discover that myths always point to our inner lives and our potential for God-realization.

Adolf Bastian, a nineteenth-century medical doctor who thought much about the human psyche, argued for the "psychic unity of mankind," meaning that the human mind, regardless of race, gender, culture, etc., operates on a shared set of "elementary ideas"

(*Elementargedanken*). Different cultures will create different flavors of these elementary ideas that Bastian called "folk ideas" (*Völkergedanken*). By studying the folk ideas of a given people, we gain insight into the elementary ideas of the human species, and in so doing come to understand what Bastian called the soul of the species (*Gesellschaftsseele*).

In *The Angelic Way* we will interpret specific angel stories as folk ideas of one spiritual tradition or another in the hopes of uncovering the greater elementary concepts underlying all angel stories, as well as the world soul in which those elementary concepts dwell and out of which each human mind emerges.

The angel stories in this book are mythic in nature. But they are not the same as legend, saga, fable, or fairy tale. While these may contain elements of myth, their purpose is to entertain and in some cases educate, while the purpose of myth is to bring about a transformation in the person wrestling with that myth. What happened to the hero in a myth can happen to us if we internalize the myth and recognize the hero's journey as our own—a journey from I to Thou and beyond.

Ultimately we are discovering that God is not a Being separate from us. The revelation is coming from within us, from that deepest and most inclusive sense that realizes that I and Thou are both manifestations of the singular Source and Substance of all reality which we may call God. Angels are imaginative faculties/capacities of ourselves that can lift the I-It of our ego-centered minds into the I-Thou of world-centered soul, and then lead both toward the I-I of God-centered spirit. Our myths are calling us to realize the truth of the revelation of the sixth-century BCE *Chandogya Upanishad*: *Tat tvam asi*—"You are that; you are God."[9]

One

Angels through the Ages

❧

OUR SEARCH FOR angels begins with the ancient Persian prophet Zoroaster (or Zarathushtra), whose origins are still debated among scholars, with dates ranging from 1500 BCE to the sixth century BCE. This may surprise those who associate angels primarily with the Bible, but in fact angels rarely appear in the oldest texts of the Bible—and when they do, they are unnamed messengers of God.

Named angels who act independently of God do not appear until the book of Daniel in the Hebrew Bible and the noncanonical *Book of Enoch*, both of which achieved their final form during the Hellenistic period of the Maccabean revolt against the Syro-Hellenes around 165 BCE. But both books had started to take form hundreds of years earlier during the Babylonian exile of the Jews beginning in 586 BCE, and it was there that the Jews were introduced to a sophisticated angelology derived from Zoroastrianism.

Zoroaster was originally a reform-minded priest of the ancient religion of the Magi. He founded a new faith that came to dominate the Persian Empire from the sixth century BCE to the Muslim conquest of Persia (today's Iran) in the mid-seventh century CE.

Scripturally, the heart of Zoroastrianism consists of five Gathas, or songs, composed by Zoroaster in Avestan, a close linguistic cousin to Sanskrit. The Gathas tell us that *Ahura Mazda*, the Lord of Light, transcends the world and yet has intimate and constant contact with humanity. The means of this contact are the seven attributes of Ahura Mazda: *Vohu Manah*/Good Thought, *Asha Vahishta*/Justice and Truth, *Ksharthra Vairya*/Dominion, *Spenta Armaiti*/Devotion and Serenity, *Haurvatat*/Wholeness, *Ameretat*/Immortality, and *Sraosa*, the messenger of Ahura Mazda who also guides the dead to the afterlife.

These seven attributes are called *Amesha Spentas*, the Bounteous Immortals—they are precursors of the archangels in the Abrahamic traditions of Judaism, Christianity, and Islam. Each of the Amesha Spentas is said to have an aspect of the created world for which it is responsible: Vohu Manah watches over animals, Asha Vahishta controls fire and energy, Ksharthra Vairya is associated with metals and minerals, Spenta Armaiti is connected with earth and land, Haurvatat is linked to water, Ameretat focuses on plants, and Sraosa brings the divine message to humankind.

The first three Immortals were thought to be male, the next three female. The gender of the seventh is unknown. The goal of the believer is to imitate the qualities articulated by the Amesha Spentas, and not simply to call upon them for help.

The link between Ahura Mazda and his seven attributes is not all that clear. The Amesha Spentas are both aspects of the One God and attendant deities who, in and of themselves, are worthy of worship. Further, unlike the fully transcendent Ahura Mazda, the Amesha Spentas are found in the world of matter. The worship of the Amesha Spentas allowed critics of Zoroastrianism to claim that its followers had abandoned the monotheism of Zoroaster, but the believers countered by saying that since the Amesha Spentas were not separate from Ahura Mazda, worshipping them was worshipping him.

Zoroastrianism is often associated with dualism. While this is not altogether wrong, it is often expanded beyond what Zoroastrianism itself teaches. In the Gathas we find *Spenta Mainyu*, the Creative Energy, or Spirit, governing humanity, struggling with *Angra Mainyu*, the Hostile Spirit, the evil force.

Angra Mainyu is not at first a proper subject, but rather a state of mind. *Mainyu* is the ancient Persian word for "mind," and angra means "destructive." From our perspective this makes perfect sense. When our minds are locked in destructive patterns of thought we are opposed to the light of love and justice that is our higher self, our God-centered spirit, symbolized in Zoroastrianism as Ahura Mazda, the Lord of Light and his attributes. But over time what was first understood as the shadow side of human thought became projected onto the cosmos as the archenemy of the Lord of Light. (We will see this again in greater detail when we look at the fallen angel, Satan.) These later Zoroastrian teachers externalized the conflict between good and evil, seeing the world divided between two cosmic powers fighting each other: *Armazd* (another, later, name for Ahura Mazda) and *Ahriman* (Angra Mainyu, elevated to the role of evil twin of the Lord of Light). They also added to the numbers of angels inhabiting the Zoroastrian universe. Chief among these are the *Yazata* (Those Who Are Worthy of Worship).

The Yazata are not mentioned in any of Zoroaster's Gathas. They are, in fact, the gods of pre-Zoroastrian religions that were brought into Zoroastrianism by converts. Rather than abandon their old gods, these new believers transformed them into angels subordinate to the archangelic Amesha Spentas.

By the time the Jewish people were taken into Babylonia in chains, a rich angel tradition was flourishing there. Gradually the Jews assimilated the angelology of Zoroastrianism into their own faith.

Judaism

As mentioned, angels rarely appear in the older books of the Hebrew Bible, and they are unnamed and lack a will of their own. They are servants of God who carry out the will of God and never go against it. The Bible is clear that angels are not to be worshipped: "Manoah spoke to the angel of YHVH, 'Permit us to delay you, and cook a meal of lamb for you.' The angel of YHVH replied, 'Even if you delay me, I cannot eat your food. If you wish to present a burnt offering, then present it to YHVH'" (Judges 13:15–16).

Two types of angels are found in the Hebrew Bible: those angels who often appear in human guise, carrying out a mission from God, and those who remain with God in heaven and whose duty it is to serve and praise him. These servant angels are divided into three categories: *seraphim* (Isaiah 6:2), *cherubim* (Ezekiel 10:3), and *hayyot* (Ezekiel 1:5).

What we know of the seraphim comes from the Prophet Isaiah: "Above it stood the seraphim, each with six wings: two covered his face, two covered his feet, and two he used to fly. Each angel cried to the others saying, 'Holy, holy, holy, is YHVH, master of multitudes; the whole earth teems with his splendor'" (Isaiah 6:2–3).

Of the cherubim the Hebrew Bible tells us that they guard the gate to the Garden of Eden (Genesis 3:24), decorate the cover of the Ark of the Covenant (Exodus 25:18), appear in Ezekiel's vision (Ezekiel 10:4), and as figures made from olive wood in Solomon's Temple (1 Kings 6:23).

Hayyot are central to Ezekiel's vision of the Throne or Chariot of God: "As I looked, a windstorm blew out of the north; a huge bright cloud of endlessly flashing fire surrounded by brilliant light, and something in the center of the fire gleamed like amber. In the middle of that appeared something like four living creatures [hayyot]. Their form seemed humanlike. Each had four faces, and each had four wings . . . As for their faces, each had the face of a human, and to its right the face of a lion, and to its left the face of an ox, and the face of an eagle" (Ezekiel 1:4–10).

Our concern is mostly with those angels who interact with humans, because they are the ones who speak metaphorically of our capacity to move from ego-centered to world-centered and finally to God-centered levels of consciousness.

The prophetic writings of Ezekiel and Zechariah, who lived during the Babylonian exile and were influenced by Zoroastrian angelology, are filled with the presence of angels. Pre-exilic prophets like Isaiah and Hosea, on the other hand, know almost nothing of angels. Indeed angels appear only twice in the writings of the pre-exilics, once in Isaiah (6:2–7) and once in Hosea (12:5–6). It is not hard to see how angels came into Judaism largely through the influence of Zoroastrianism in Persia. Indeed, the Talmudic rabbis say as much when they admit that the names of the angels were brought back to Israel by the Jews who had been exiled to Babylonia (Jerusalem Talmud, tractate *Rosh haShanah*, 1:2).

There is a large increase of angels in Jewish literature written after the Babylonian exile. Jewish books created after the exile that did not make it into the Hebrew Bible, such as *Enoch, Jubilees*, and *Tobit*, are teeming with angels. The mostly second-century BCE *Book of Enoch*, which we will explore at greater length later, names seven archangels: Uriel, Raguel, Michael, Seraqael, Gabriel, Haniel, and Raphael. The *Book of Jubilees*, written sometime in the first century BCE, claims to have been dictated to Moses on Mount Sinai by an angel who revealed to Moses that there are angels of fire, winds, clouds, hail, and other natural phenomenon, as well as angels in charge of the seasons, months, weeks, and days (*Jubilees* 2:2). And the second-century BCE *Book of Tobit* is a long narrative featuring the angel Raphael who accompanies and guides the son of Tobit on an adventure.

It is primarily from these books that we learn the names of angels and archangels and get the first real introduction to fallen angels and Satan.

The early rabbis took angels for granted and, as we shall see, told many stories about them, yet there is no mention of angels in the Mishnah, the earliest law code of the rabbis compiled around the year 200 CE. Rabbinic myths from the same period are filled with angels, but it is unclear whether the rabbis took these as actual entities or metaphors for various ideas and ideals.

As Judaism developed along more philosophic and rationalistic lines, stories of angels decreased and the understanding of them became more metaphoric. The Spanish Jewish philosopher and poet Judah HaLevi (1075–1141) understood angels to be metaphors for the various laws of nature by which God governs the world. Ibn Ezra (1092–1167), who may have left Spain with Judah HaLevi for North Africa to avoid persecution, held that angels were metaphors for Platonic forms, the eternal ideas on which all material form is modeled.

On the other hand Jewish mysticism is replete with angels, seeing them as the means by which the fully transcendent God maintains contact with the world and the humans who inhabit it.

Christianity

Early Christianity inherited the Jewish world of angels and developed it further. The book of Revelation in the New Testament, for example, written sometime at the close of the first century CE by John of Patmos, and most likely influenced by the prophecy and vision of Ezekiel, tells us that cherubim, like the seraphim, are six-winged creatures whose bodies are covered with open eyes. Gabriel and Raphael, who later become archangels in other tales, are assigned to the order of the cherubim in Revelation, as is Lucifer/Satan.

The seven archangels named in *Enoch* may have been on John's mind when he mentions seven unnamed angels in Revelation 8:2: "And I saw the seven angels who stand before God, and seven trumpets were given to them."

Perhaps the most elaborate angelology is set out by Thomas Aquinas (1225–1274). According to Aquinas, angels are an absolute necessity in God's creation. God's love is such that God desires beings who can imitate him—and angels are those beings. Both God and angels are pure intelligence, having nothing material about them. Humans, being made of matter, cannot imitate God as fully as angels.

As the literary critic and Bible scholar Harold Bloom writes, "The great Thomistic insight is that angels have perfect knowledge of their own spirituality and so of their own freedom."[1] Angels as spirit intelligences represent that aspect of human consciousness that will set us free from the limits of ego-centered thinking and the I-It world view. As Bloom says,

> His (Thomas Aquinas's) angels occupy the gap between the human mind and the mind of God, and he reasoned that without the angels such a divide never could be bridged. Hierarchy required a chain of being, with differences in kind as well as degree distinguishing angels and humans. Since Aquinas subtly argued that God was (and is) free to create universes other than ours, and indeed more perfect than ours, the great theologian, for the honor of our cosmos, argued also that elements of pure spirit had been created by God for it. Angels, though awesome and terrible, are thus complements to us, and enhance our dignity.[2]

This is central to our argument. Angels are complements to humanity; they are the way we humans can become fully human, overcoming our ego-centered mind to which we all too often limit ourselves and our self-understanding.

Aquinas's fascination with angels may have stemmed from the compelling nature of the writings of a late fifth- or early sixth-century CE author who took the pseudonym Dionysius the Areopagite. The original Dionysius the Areopagite is mentioned in the New

Testament in the book of Acts (17:34), where he is identified as an Athenian who converted to Christianity under Paul the Apostle. Five centuries later a Neoplatonist assumed the name Dionysius the Areopagite (scholars refer to him as Pseudo-Dionysius) and wrote *The Celestial Hierarchy*, a work on angelology that has shaped official Christian thought on angels ever since.

According to Pseudo-Dionysius there are three hierarchies of angels, each of them containing three orders of angels. Beginning with the highest hierarchy, he lists *Seraphim*, the caretakers of God's throne who chant, "Holy, holy, holy, is YHVH, master of multitudes; the whole earth teems with his splendor" (Isaiah 6:3); *Cherubim*, the guardians of the way back to the Garden of Eden (Genesis 3:24); and *Thrones*, living symbols of God's justice mentioned in the letter to the Colossians (1:16). The next hierarchy includes *Dominions*, who regulate the activity of the angels; *Virtues*, who regulate the stars and planets in heaven; and *Powers*, warrior angels tasked with keeping history and conscience. The third hierarchy contains *Principalities*, who carry out the directives of the Dominions; *Archangels*, the seven senior angels; and *Angels* themselves, messengers from the divine to the human.

Islam

Since Islam is the third of the Abrahamic religions, it is not surprising that angels play a part in it no less than in Judaism and Christianity. Here is the most concise Islamic statement of belief regarding angels:

> We must confess that God has angels who act according to His order, and who do not rebel against Him.

They neither eat nor drink, nor is there amongst them any difference of sex. They are on earth, and in heaven. Some have charge of men and record their actions. Some angels are high in stature and are possessed of great power. Such a one is *Jibra'il* who in the space of one hour descends from heaven to earth, and who with one wing can lift up a mountain.

We must believe in *'Izra'il*, who receives the souls of men when they die, and in *Israfil*, into whose charge is committed the trumpet. When he receives the order, he will blow such a terrible blast that all living things will die. This is the commencement of the last day.[3]

While no mention is made here of the angel *Mika'il* (Michael), he does play a role in Islam as the caretaker of the physical needs of humankind. Mika'il, Jibril (Gabriel), Israfil (Raphael), and 'Izra'il (Azrael) are archangels who, in their many guises in Judaism, Christianity, and Islam, will occupy much of our book.

All angels are servants of Allah and share one primary purpose, and that is to praise him: "Everyone in the heavens and earth belongs to Him, and those that are with Him are never too proud to worship Him, nor do they grow weary; they glorify Him tirelessly night and day" (Qur'an 21:19–20).[4] "Those [angels] who carry the Throne and those who surround it celebrate the praise of their Lord and have faith in Him. They beg forgiveness for the believers . . ." (Qur'an 40:7).[5]

According to Islam, there are times when angels appear in human form, but they are usually without form and invisible to human beings. With regard to humans, the angels act as guardians; the

Qur'an teaches: "each person has guardian angels before him and behind, watching over him by God's command . . ." (Qur'an 13:11).⁶ The number of guardian angels can be quite large: "Remember when you said to the believers, 'Will you be satisfied if your Lord reinforces you by sending down three thousand angels? Well, if you are steadfast and mindful of God, your Lord will reinforce you with five thousand swooping angels if the enemy should suddenly attack you!' . . ." (Qur'an 3:124–125).⁷ And the guardian angels will stay with a person all through life: "He is the Supreme Master over His subjects. He sends out recorders to watch over you until, when death overtakes any of you, those sent by Us take his soul—they never fail in their duty" (Qur'an 6:61).⁸

The Hadith (82.10), Islam's tradition that focuses on the teachings and deeds of the Prophet Muhammad, says that two angels watch over a person by day, and two others by night. These angels who stand to the right and left side of a person are called *Mua'qqibat*, "those who succeed one another," because they take turns standing guard, and *Kiraman Katibin*, the "illustrious recorders," because they record all the deeds a person performs. As Kiraman Katibin these angels are mentioned in the Qur'an: "Do they think We cannot hear their secret talk and their private counsel? Yes we can: Our messengers are at their sides, recording everything" (Qur'an 43:80).⁹

The angel to our right is more merciful than the angel to our left, and seeks to prevent the stricter angel from overreacting to our errors and foibles. According to the Hadith, when the strict angel is about to record some deed of ours, the merciful angel dissuades him, saying, "Wait a little for seven hours; perhaps he will pray and ask pardon."¹⁰

While our guardian angels remain unnamed in Islam, there are other named angels in addition to the four archangels. *Ridwan* is in charge of Paradise, and *Malik* presides over Hell. According to Abu Hamid Muhammad al-Ghazali (1058–1111), one of Islam's greatest philosophers, two frightening-looking black angels named *Munkar* and *Nakir* visit the dead the first night they are in their graves. They call the dead to sit up in body and soul that they might question them, "Who is your Lord, and what is your religion, and who is your prophet?"[11]

Distinct from angels in Islam, and yet often mistaken for them, are the *jinn* (genii). According to the Qur'an the jinn were created thousands of years before Adam, the first human: "We created man out of dried clay formed from dark mud—the jinn We created before, from the fire of scorching wind" (Qur'an 15:26–27).[12] Like humans and unlike angels, the jinn eat, drink, procreate, and die, though they can live hundreds of years. Their greatest desire is to hear the Qur'an recited. Perhaps the most well-known of the jinn is *Iblis*, the Islamic version of Satan.

Candomblé

Even though angels are most pronounced in Judaism, Christianity, and Islam, angel-like beings occur in other traditions as well. While mindful of the differences among indigenous peoples and their beliefs, the Afro-Brazilian religion of Candomblé provides a representative model of angel-like beings among indigenous religions.

Candomblé is an amalgam of African and Brazilian traditions, and is practiced primarily in Brazil. According to this faith there exists an all-powerful creator God, *Olorun*, who created not only the heavens and the earth, but myriads of beings who occupy realms between these two. Unlike God in Judaism, Christianity, and Islam, Olorun is not a person, and one cannot have a personal relationship with Olorun. Though an impersonal force, Olorun is kind and beneficent, and it is out of his abundant mercy that Olorun formed angels to assist humanity and to govern nature. These angels are called *orishas*, and manifest as both male and female.

Each human being is assigned a father and mother orisha at birth whose task it is to protect and guide him or her throughout life. Each orisha is associated with one aspect of nature, and to discover their orisha parents Candomblé followers pay close attention to nature to discover which aspects of it speak to them the loudest. These aspects are associated with specific places, called power spots, and these power spots are thought to be the home of a person's orisha parents.

Visiting power spots puts people in contact with their orishas. Power spots are not specific locations as much as generic ones. That is to say, while a specific lake may resonate with an individual and reveal itself to be his or her power spot and home to his or her orisha, once this is discovered any lake can act as a doorway to the home of that person's orisha.

Is there an angel-human connection in the Candomblé faith that allows for our interpretation of angels as metaphors? As we have seen, orishas function as guardian angels, to borrow a term from the West, but there is a more intimate connection. Followers of Candomblé believe *Oshala* (*Oxala*) is the father of all the orishas and also the grandfather of all human beings. Oshala's wife, *Nanan* (*Nana*) is the *vovo* or grandmother of humanity. Orishas/angels and humans derive from the same source, Oshala and Nanan, suggesting that we share a common heritage and nature—an idea that supports our notion that the angelic resides within the human.

Hinduism

Hinduism has no named angels. *Devas*, from the Sanskrit root *div*, to shine, are "luminous energy principles behind all phenomena,"[13] closer in concept to the orishas than to the angels of the Abrahamic traditions. In Western parlance they are often referred to as "gods," but this suggests a polytheism that the Veda, the ancient collection of Hindu scriptures, denies.

The Vedas (from the Sanskrit *veda*, "knowledge") are the oldest sacred texts of Hinduism. The oldest of the Vedas, the Rig Veda, was most likely compiled from earlier oral teachings beginning about 1500 BCE. The Vedas are said to be *apauruseva*, "not of human origin," and were transmitted to the sages by God. They are also called *sruti*, "what is heard."

There are four canonical Vedas called Samhitas. They are the Rig Veda, 1028 hymns to the gods; the Yajur Veda, a collection of readings, many adapted from the Rig Veda, used in sacrificial rites; Sama Veda, an anthology of 1549 songs (*sama* comes from the Sanskrit word *saman*, "melody"), all but 78 of which come from the Rig Veda; and the Atharva Veda, which consists of magical spells and cosmological and speculative hymns to *Skambha* (the causal principle of life), *Prana* (the Breath of Life), and others.

According to the Vedas the devas are the workings of the singular *Tat*, "That," the one that "breathes windless by its own impulse" (Rig Veda X.129.2).[14] This is the unknowable God beyond all human thought: "That which is beyond the sky and beyond this earth and beyond the gods" (Rig Veda X.82.5).[15]

Because this One contains all potentiality and possibility, its nature is to manifest both in a multitude of forms, which the Western world would call creation. But, unlike in the West where creation is an artifact created by God as a potter might fashion a pot, in India creation is the body of God and not something separate from God.

The unfolding of the One (*tad ekam*) manifests first as the devas, the "Life-Light-Intelligence" of all phenomena, both micro- and macrocosmic.[16] The devas are the ordering principles of the universe, "law abiding, born in law, sublime fosterers of law, haters of falsehood" (Rig Veda VII.66.13ab).[17] The intelligence that is the devas lays out the map of creation and then manifests it as the myriad phenomena of the cosmos.

Unlike angels in Zoroastrianism, Judaism, Christianity, and Islam, the devas are not sent as messengers from God, but rather principles of God that order life, including human life. If the devas do not seek out humankind, however, humans can seek out the devas.

The *rishis*, or poet-seers of Vedic India, discovered that devas could be encountered through a blend of chant and imagination. An example is this prayer to *Agni*, the Lord of Fire who acts as a messenger between humanity and the gods, and hence functions in a manner not unlike angels: "O Tireless Knower of generations! Bring us the prolific word that it may shine to heaven" (Rig Veda VI.16.36).[18] The word in this case is a *mantra*, a syllable, word, or phrase that, when repeated over and over again, attunes the mind to the frequency of the deva to whom it is addressed. Once attuned, the chanter and the deva "dance" together, each opened to the other as aspects of the Greater One that is God.

For the rishis, attuning themselves to the devas allowed the devas to appear to humans in visions. "There, where the birds vigilantly sing forth their share of immortality, the lordly herdsman of the whole universe, the enlightened One, has entered into me, the simple" (Rig Veda I.164.21).[19]

The unity of devas with humanity parallels the unity of Candomblé orishas with humanity. As the seer or shaman invokes the deity without, he or she discovers it manifest within. Indeed, the very idea of "in" and "out" is no longer perceived as discrete points, but as a seamless spectrum. The Western idea of angels provides the same realization of an unbroken chain of being.

The visions of the rishis are not fixed, and the devas do not appear in consistent and predictable form. As their name implies they are shining, luminescent, and unformed. Like the orishas, devas are seen as the manifestations of a natural force, like Dawn, Fire, Wind, Sun, or *Soma*, the sacred plant and drink.

Since devas are not messengers from God but manifestations of God, they are not here to aid humanity; they exist to ensure that there is a "here" in the first place. And because they are the "here"— the Whole, of which we are a part—devas are not separate from humanity: "Having poured together the whole mortal, the gods entered man" (Atharva Veda XI.8.13.cd).[20]

The devas are within us, those aspects of us that lead beyond the ego-centered mind toward God-centered spirit. Thus, while in no way conflating devas with angels, both point to the same human capacity to broaden one's consciousness beyond the I-It and ultimately toward the I-I. In the words of the scholar Jeanine Miller,

> The subtle characteristics of the devas and their reflections in the human psyche were expressed in the Vedas, on the whole, in terms of the powers of Nature, because of humankind's close communion with Nature. Nature is the phenomenal expression of the devas' activity. We cannot dissociate the one from the

other. But human beings are also the playground of this same activity. The interblending of the devas' influences reflects an intimate relationship with the human psyche's weaving of its own destiny. From our modern psychological standpoint, the devas appear as variations on the one theme of the pilgrim's perpetual search for light, understanding, achievement and enlightenment, his or her ascent and descent, struggling, questioning and finding. Each deva mirrors and confers on the worshipper something of itself . . .[21]

Buddhism

Devas also found their way into Buddhism, a reformist movement within Hinduism founded by Siddhartha Gotama, a Northern Indian prince who became the Awakened One, the *Buddha*, some 2500 years ago.

As in Hinduism, the Buddhist devas are by and large invisible to all humans except those who have cultivated the spiritual insight to peer into nonhuman planes of existence. They are also inaudible except to those who have mastered the art of hearing the voices coming from the nonhuman realms. If a deva wishes to be seen and heard, it must conjure an illusory form that is perceptible to human senses.

Buddhist cosmology, the main outlines of which seem to have been synthesized in the third century BCE, holds that the devas reside in three realms, the *Arupyadhatu*, the *Rupadhatu*, and the *Kamadhatu*, each of which can be divided into numerous subworlds.

Arupyadhatu is the Formless Realm, and the devas in this realm are of four types. The first is *Naivasa jnanasa jnayatana*. These are intelligences who no longer perceive separate beings or things at all, and yet are not completely unaware of their own existence. According to Buddhist tradition the second teacher of the Buddha, Udraka Ramaputra, attained this state of enlightenment and dwelt as a deva in this realm.

The second type of devas in the Formless Realm is *Aki canyayatana*, "Those Who Lack Nothing." These are devas who continually contemplate the thought, but have not yet realized the truth of the thought, that there are no separate beings or things in existence. The Buddha's first teacher, Arada Kalama, was thought to live at this level of attainment.

Vijnananantyayatana, the third type of devas, focuses on the infinite nature of its own consciousness, while *Akasanantyayatana*, the fourth type of devas, dwells on the limitlessness of space.

The bodyless devas of the Formless Realm have little interaction with humans, absorbed as they are in their own contemplations. Things are a bit different when we look at the devas of the *Rupadhatu*, the Form Realm.

Here the devas each have bodies and exist in time and space, though these bodies are still invisible to us humans. Devas of the Form Realm do not experience pleasure or pain, have no sensory desires, or gender distinctions. There are five kinds of *Rupadhatu* devas.

The *Suddhavasa* devas were originally Buddhist monks (and perhaps nuns) who died before achieving full enlightenment or the state of *Arhat*, "worthy one," someone who has seen through the delusions of ego-centered existence, but not yet into the full consciousness of Buddha mind, or what we are calling God-centered spirit. These devas guard and protect Buddhism on earth, and will, in time, achieve the level of Arhat.

The next layer "down" is the sphere of the *Bhatphala* devas. These are beings who rest in a state of pure tranquility, a state the Buddha called a subtle form of happiness. A bit lower than these devas are the *Subhaktsna* devas who rest in a joyous state. Below them are the *Abhasvara* devas who exist without any movement of thought whatsoever. And yet lower are the *Brahma* devas who can think only wholesome thoughts. The *Brahma* devas are interested in, and can become engaged with, the human realm (thus functioning more like the angels of the Abrahamic religions) by intervening in the lives of people to offer advice and counsel. The "difficulty" with the *Brahma* devas is that they are often ignorant of the higher spheres and imagine that they are the creators of the worlds below them.

In addition to these devas in the Formless Realm and the Form Realm there are those of the *Kamadhatu* realm, especially the human-like *Parinirmita-vasavartin* devas, the most famous of whom is *Mara*, the Tempter, who plays a roll in the story of the Buddha's enlightenment not unlike Satan in the testing of Jesus in the wilderness.

Overall the Buddha refrained from speaking about devas and gods, but there is one exception that relates directly to our subject. Chapter 10 of the *Aggañña Sutta*, an early Pali text, includes a conversation between two Brahmins who became Buddhist monks, and who spoke with the Buddha about the origins of the universe. Speaking to Vasettha, one of the Brahmins, the Buddha said,

> There comes a time, Vasettha, when, sooner or later
> after a long period, this world [the human world] con-
> tracts. At a time of contraction, beings are mostly born
> [as devas] in the Abhassara Brahma world [the Realm
> of Radiance]. And there they dwell, mind-made,

feeding on delight, self-luminous, moving through the air, glorious—and they stay like that for a very long time. But sooner or later, after a very long period, this world [the human world] begins to expand again. At a time of expansion, the beings [devas] from the Abhassara Brahma world, having passed away from there, are mostly reborn in this world [as humans once again].[22]

What is striking about Buddhist devas is that they were once humans. What is even more striking is that in time devas become humans once more. The world we experience is filled with devas, and they are us! This unity of humans and devas speaks directly to our premise that angels are aspects of our human imagination, perhaps even the imagination itself when it is applied to opening the seemingly separate ego to the nondual reality of the greater whole.

• • •

The universality of angels and angelic equivalents attests to the fact that the capacity for humans to transcend their ego-centered consciousness and attain higher and more inclusive levels of awareness is perennial and global. People in all times and of all cultures have wished, to use a Western image, to take wing and fly higher. The higher we fly the more inclusive our vision becomes—we can see what earth-bounded eyes cannot. And what we come to see when we ascend high enough is that the whole universe is a single system of interconnected lives who, we realize at the highest point in our journey, are all manifestations of the One Being, God.

A complete survey of angels, orishas, devas, and similar beings in all the world's religious traditions would go far beyond both the scope and the focus of this book. Based on our understanding that angels are not beings separate from us, but capacities within us, and that myths about angels can show us the way, we will in the following chapters mostly explore three major groups of angelic beings: first those angels who especially interact with humans—like Michael, Gabriel, Raphael, Uriel, Satan, and the angel of death—as they appear in Judaism, Christianity, and Islam; then humans who have become angels; and finally humans who have, with the aid of angels, risen to the highest heavens and then returned to earth to guide others in their quest to realize their own God-centered spirit.

Two

Angelic Imagination

❧

WHILE ANGEL-LIKE begins can be found in many religious traditions, angels themselves seem to be a uniquely Western idea. When we think of angels the images that come to mind are those of Zoroastrianism, Judaism, Christianity, and Islam. And it will be from these traditions, though primarily the later three, that we will draw most of our examples.

Of the three Abrahamic faiths, Judaism is the oldest, and through the Hebrew Bible and its accompanying rabbinic commentary, it is Judaism that provides many of the root myths that find new expression and meaning in Christianity and Islam. Thus we will use early

Jewish angel stories as our starting place for exploring angels in general.

To read angel myths and stories with an eye to their deeper psycho-spiritual meaning requires a certain mind-set. In Judaism this mind-set is called *midrashic*, "investigative," and the body of work this mind-set creates is called *midrash*.

The Hebrew word *midrash* comes from the word *drash*, "to inquire," and refers to oral and written teachings that bring out the deeper meanings of scripture. There are two types of midrash, *midrash halacha* that explicate the Bible's legal code (*halacha*), and *midrash aggadah*, myths and legends (*aggadah/aggadot*) that deal with theology and ethics. When dealing with angels it is the latter that is of interest to us.

While there is evidence of *midrash aggadah* in early rabbinic writings, the form explodes in popularity sometime in the third century CE and maintains its popularity for a thousand years. Unlike *midrash halacha*, which because of its legal nature tends toward tight logic, *midrash aggadah* invites the free play of the imagination. Biblical tales are retold with details added from the imagination of the teller.

Here we will be guided by the classic *midrash aggadah* of the rabbis found in the collection called *Midrash Rabbah*, the Great Midrash. This compilation of rabbinic myths and legends is difficult to date since different myths were composed at different times. Generally speaking, however, the earliest myths are those found in the first volume of the collection, *Genesis Rabbah* (literally the "Great Genesis," but better understood as "The Great Collection of Myths Based on Genesis"), which was completed some time in the fifth century CE, and which contains myths that date back at least two centuries. The latest compilations of *Midrash Rabbah* are from the ninth century CE, but here, too, the myths themselves are much older than the date of their compilation.

The authors of midrash take the original biblical story as a catalyst for their own imaginative play. This is important to remember throughout our book. We are dealing not with the Bible as codified in Judaism, Catholicism, Eastern Orthodoxy, or Protestantism, but with the Bible as grist for imaginative rabbinic play. One need not ask of these myths, "Is that in the Bible?" for the answer is always the same—"No." The proper question is rather, "Where in this myth is the seed of the original Bible tale?"

To see how midrash works, let's begin with the biblical story of the creation of humanity: "Then God said, 'Let us fashion humanity in our image in harmony with our likeness' . . . So God created humanity in the divine image, in the image of the divine he created them; masculine and feminine he created them" (Genesis 1:26–27).

The story, if it can even be called a story, is sparse and terse. We know nothing of what was going on in the mind of God, or to whom God was speaking when God said, "Let us fashion." This is where the rabbinic imagination enters: "When the blessed Holy One desired— when it arose in His will—to create the world, He gazed into Torah [the heavenly version of revelation that comes to earth as the Five Books of Moses] and created it . . . As He was about to create *adam* ['earthling' from *adamah*, 'earth'], Torah exclaimed: 'If a human being is created and then proceeds to sin, and You punish him—why should the Work of Your hands be in vain, since he will be unable to endure Your judgment?' YHVH replied, 'I have already prepared *teshuvah*, returning [remorse or conscience] before creating the world.'"[1]

Torah fears that God is wasting time creating the world if God intends to place humankind in it. Humans will sin, God will be obligated to punish them, and the magnitude of that punishment will obliterate the world—making the act of creation a cosmic waste of time. This would be true if God had not already taken precaution.

Before the creation of humanity and, by extension, sin, God created *teshuvah*, repentance. Literally *teshuvah* means "return," implying that when one sins one turns away from one's true nature and true path, and that repentance is returning to that true nature and path. The drama that captivates God, the drama God anticipated from before the first moment of humanity's creation, the drama hinted at in Psalm 8 (see page 9) that brings God back time and again to remember and visit us mortals is this: How will humans turn away—and how will they find their way back? This is the key to all great drama, whether it is played out on a stage, on the pages of a book, on a screen—or on earth. Falling away from truth and returning to it is the very heart of the human adventure, and this drama is as compelling to God as it is to us.

Over two thousand years after the psalmist raised the issue of why God bothers with humans, the rabbis debated the relative greatness of angels and Israelites. While Psalm 8 makes it clear that humanity as a whole is a little lower than the angels, could it be that Israelites, being the chosen few of humanity, have a different standing in the divine hierarchy? Could it be that while most of humanity is lower than the angels, the people Israel is a bit higher? Some rabbis argued in the affirmative, others in the negative. Rabbi Hayim of Volozhin (1749–1821) argued that both arguments were correct.

First Rabbi Volozhin narrowed the definition of Israelite to refer not to Jews in general but those individuals of any group who were disciples of Truth. Second, he affirmed that there are levels of Truth dependent upon levels of consciousness. In making this point he quoted from *Zohar Hadash* (New Zohar), the fifth volume of the thirteenth-century "Bible" of Jewish mysticism, *Sefer Zohar* (Book of Illumination), written by the Spanish kabbalist Moses de Leon (1250–1305). Moses de Leon said, "The conception of God of which angels are capable is greater than that of any creature living below the level of angelic consciousness. Below the consciousness of angels is that of the heavens, and this surpasses any conception of God those below the heavens can conceive. Below this is the lowest level of consciousness, the level of the human, those grounded in dust, which despite its low level is still greater than anything below it can imagine."[2]

Rabbi Volozhin imagined a hierarchy of consciousness and used that hierarchy to argue for the supremacy of angels over humans. Angels operate at such a high level of consciousness that they are able to imagine God far more accurately than we humans can. In this they are higher than humans. But, he continued, there is something humans have that angels lack, and this is what makes humanity rank higher than angels: "An angel is in essence only one individual power, in which there is no generalization of all the several worlds. Hence it is in no way within the power of angels to elevate, join together, or unify any world with the one spread above their heads, for they have no part in common with them . . . Humanity alone elevates, joins and unifies the Worlds and their Light by virtue of human deeds, inasmuch as the human is comprised of all of these worlds."[3]

In other words, angels have the capacity to transcend lower levels, but without humans to embody that capacity they are totally ineffective. This makes them lower than humans, for even if humans do not move from ego-centered mind to world-centered soul (let alone

God-centered spirit) they can still do good deeds here on earth, something angels cannot do. Humans, even without using their angelic faculties, still have something to offer; angels without humans, however, are nothing at all. As Rabbi Volozhin wrote, "Thus even an angel can feel an elevation and an addition to his sanctity coming from [a person] as a result of human deeds, *since the angel is virtually a component part of man* [emphasis added]. And even the soul of man is devoid of this exalting and unifying power until it descends into the world of action in the human body. So it is written: 'He blew the breath of life into his nostrils'—a soul to all the worlds . . ."[4]

• • •

Angels are components of human consciousness. They are personifications of human capacities for knowing and achieving higher and more inclusive levels of awareness. The angelic as part of the human is an insight the ancient rabbis found buried in the biblical story of Jacob's ladder.

Escaping from the murderous rage of his brother, Esau, Jacob races toward Haran, the place where his grandfather Abraham had lived before he journeyed to Canaan, and where Jacob hopes to find safety and shelter with his maternal uncle, Laban, who lives there now. "Jacob departed from Beer-sheba and traveled toward Haran. As the sun set he found a place to camp for the night, and arranging stones as pillows for his head, he lay down to sleep. And he dreamt: And a ladder was set on the earth with its top reaching into the heavens, and angels of God were ascending and descending on it" (Genesis 28:10–12).

Before engaging the midrash associated with this dream, it is useful to note that we are dealing with a Jewish version of a universal mythic theme. The ladder appears in many traditions. It is the Siberian shaman's tent pole that he climbs to draw nearer to heaven. It is the *klimax* of the mysteries of Mithra, the pre-Zoroastrian religion of Persia, a ladder made of the seven planetary metals that each initiate was given to climb. It is the Babylonian ziggurat climbed to reach the heavens. It is the ladder of Taiwanese Taoists and Japanese *Yamabushi* ascetics who climb a ladder made of razor-sharp swords. The ladder motif also exists in some understandings of Muhammad's Night Journey, and it can be found in parts of Africa where it is thought to link spirits and gods with people. A variation on the ladder is told among the native peoples of North America. The Algonquin, for example, speak of a hero, Tchakabech, who climbs to heaven via a giant tree to meet the sun god.

To imagine Jacob's dream to be unique to the Bible is to miss the power of this myth. The ancient rabbis, of course, knew nothing of Yamabushi monks and Siberian shamans, yet they knew that they were dealing with something beyond a mere material ladder.

The first question the rabbis asked was why are the angels seen ascending and descending rather than descending and ascending? If angels originate in heaven and are sent down to earth to fulfill some mission, one would expect to see them coming down first, and climbing up only after their task is complete. According to the midrash, among the ascending angels were Raphael and Gabriel, the two angels who had destroyed Sodom one hundred and thirty-eight years earlier. Because they had disclosed their mission to Lot and helped him escape, something God had not ordered them to do, they were banished by God to wander the earth for all these years. They had accompanied Jacob on his journey, and having reached Moriah, the site of the near sacrifice of Isaac, and much later of the Jerusalem Temple, they were allowed to return home.

Upon their arrival in heaven, Raphael and Gabriel called out to their fellow angels to behold the face of Jacob, whose image they said appears also on the Throne of God.[5]

What does it mean that Jacob's face appears on the Throne of God? It is again a mythic way of pointing to the unity of God and humanity.

Jacob's dream tells us that angels are a means of moving from earth to heaven and back to earth again. That is to say, angels are symbolic of the human capacity to shift from mind to soul, from I-It to I-Thou consciousness. Lest we doubt the rabbis mean to link angels to humans, the rabbis claim that the lower end of the ladder is connected to the human body.[6]

The angels in Jacob's vision both descend into and ascend up from the human body, suggesting that angels are not simply the imaginings of the human mind, but rather the human imagination itself. Angels, at least the way the rabbis viewed them, are not symbols for something else, but the source of symbol making itself. Angels are not figments of the imagination, but the capacity for imagination.

We find a further hint of this in another rabbinic myth about Jacob. In this midrash Jacob meets the angel Uriel (Light of God) who says to him, "I have descended to earth to live among humanity. My name is Jacob."[7] Jacob is meeting the Light of God who reveals himself to be another Jacob. In other words, the angelic Uriel is the human Jacob's spiritual alter ego.

According to our understanding of angels as internal forces, Uriel is saying to Jacob, "I am Uriel, the Light of Consciousness by which you see God, and through which you come to know yourself as a manifestation of God. If I am to guide you toward God, toward the realization of your own divine nature, you must follow me, and to follow me you must imagine I am not inside you but outside you. To keep you from mistaking me for someone other than your inner soul, I will take on your shape and your name, so that whenever we meet you will know you are meeting yourself."

We will draw from midrash throughout this book, but these first examples make clear the imaginative play at the heart of the midrashic mind-set.

The question arising from these two *midrashim* (plural of *midrash*) is this: What is the ultimate state toward which we are to climb when we dare to climb out of our own heads on our own ladders? Our answer is that we climb from ego-centered mind to world-centered soul to God-centered spirit.

But how did great spiritual masters articulate this same truth in the past?

When Jesus moved from I-It through I-Thou to I-I awareness he exclaimed, "The Father and I are one" (John 10:30). When the ninth-century Sufi mystic Bayazid al-Bistami did the same he said, "I am truth, I am the true God."

The following story expands on the experience of al-Bistami:

> Being [Allah, God] asked [al-Bistami], "What is the throne of Being?" He answered, "I am the throne of Being." "What is the table on which the divine decrees are written?" "I am that table." "What is the pen of God—the word by which God created all things?" "I am the pen." "What is Abraham, Moses, and Jesus?" "I am Abraham, Moses, and Jesus." "What are the angels

Gabriel, Michael, Israfil?" "I am Gabriel, Michael, Israfil, for whatever comes to true being is absorbed into God, and this [al-Bistami said, referring to himself] is God."[8]

Similarly, the great Sufi poet and teacher Jalal ad-Din Rumi (1207–1273) offered this interpretation of his own:

One knocked at the door of the Beloved, and a voice from within inquired, "Who is there?" Then he answered, "It is I." And the voice said, "This house will not hold me and thee." So the door remained shut. Then the Lover sped away into the wilderness, and fasted and prayed in solitude. And after a year he returned, and knocked again at the door, and the voice again demanded, "Who is there?" and the Lover said, "It is Thou." Then the door was opened.[9]

Who is this God these great mystics discovered? A first answer might come from the myth of Moses's encounter with God at the burning bush.

When asked by Moses to reveal his name, God replies, *Ehyeh asher Ehyeh* (Exodus 3:14). As noted earlier most English Bibles translate the Hebrew as the static "I am that I am," rather than the more accurate and intriguing "I will be whatever I will be."

God is not a static "I am," but a flowing "I will be"; not a fixed being but an eternal becoming. God is process not product, and the process is creative, unpredictable, always surprising. To say, "The Father and I are one" (John 10:30), is not to identify with a static state, but with a creative flow. God is creativity and all expressions of creativity. The nature of God is to forever create new forms, new options, new possibilities.

This too is revealed in the Hebrew Bible. Let us take for example the first of the Ten Commandments revealed to Moses: "I am YHVH your God Who has taken you out of *Mitzrayim* [the land of Egypt], from the house of bondage" (Exodus 20:2).

YHVH, another form of the Hebrew verb "to be," is the process of liberation. Liberation from what? From *Mitzrayim*, which is a Hebrew pun meaning "from the narrow places." *Mitzrayim* is both a geographical place and a state of mind. On the mythic level the Bible is saying that YHVH is the process whereby humanity is liberated from the narrow places of enslavement.

There are, of course, as many places of enslavement as there are people to imagine them, but the one narrow place in which we are all enslaved is the ego-centered mind itself and its fundamental belief that "I and God are *not* one." Angels and the angelic are expressions of human creativity pointing the way out of this (dis-)illusion.

Three

Humans and Angels

ↂↇↄↂↇↄ

IN MANY OF the great myths involving angels, the angels are mistaken for people. If we understand angels as symbolic personifications of higher and more inclusive levels of human consciousness, and stories about angels as mythic signposts pointing us toward the insights such consciousness reveals, then the reason for the blurring of the distinction between angels and humans is to remind us that angels are indeed us.

One of the clearest examples of this confusion is found in the book of Joshua, the first book of the Former Prophets in the Bible. Written by several writers during the eight and seventh centuries BCE, the book tells the story of the Israelite invasion of Canaan.

Once while in Jericho, Joshua looked to see a man standing across from him, his sword drawn in his hand. Joshua approached him and asked, "Are you one of us or one of our enemies?" And he answered, "Neither. I am the chief of the Lord's army; I have just arrived." Then Joshua prostrated to the ground and said to him, "What does my lord wish to say to his servant?" And the chief of the Lord's army said to Joshua, "Remove your shoe from your foot, for the place upon which you stand is holy"—and Joshua did so. (Joshua 5:13–15)

This is a strange story. Joshua, warlord of the Israelites, is suddenly confronted by a stranger brandishing an unsheathed sword. The defensive reflex of any soldier would be to unsheathe one's own sword, yet Joshua does not do so. Rather he asks the man to state his allegiance to Israel or to the enemy. The fact that Joshua entertains the notion that this could be a mortal enemy makes his action all the more odd, and it is the strangeness of the story that suggests we are dealing with a dream encounter rather than a waking one.

In this dream Joshua encounters his angelic self. Because the encounter is recalled from the ego's perspective, the angel appears separate from Joshua, fully human and hence bound by time and space. "I have just arrived," the angel tells Joshua as if he traveled in the manner of humans. The phrase "I have just arrived" should be understood to mean that the projection of the angelic Joshua outside the dreaming ego is happening in the moment.

The angel reveals himself as the chief of God's armies, suggesting that he is Joshua's cosmic counterpart. Joshua then asks what it is that the angel has come to say to him. One would expect the angel to say something encouraging with regard to the coming battle over Jericho. Instead he closely echoes God's words to Moses at the burning bush: "Take off the sandals from your feet" (Exodus 3:5).

The difference between the command given to Moses and that given to Joshua is subtle and significant. Moses is told to remove both sandals from both feet, Joshua is told to remove only one sandal from one foot. Given that the writer of the Joshua story is consciously linking his hero, Joshua, to his hero's mentor, Moses, why change the command from the plural in Moses's case to the singular in Joshua's case?

To find an answer we have to remember that we are dealing with mythic symbols. What do sandals represent in these encounters? Sandals are a protective barrier between the human and the earth. In Hebrew, the language of both Exodus and the book of Joshua, the link between these two is clearer than it is in the English translation.

As noted earlier, the human is _adam_, the earth is _adamah_. _Adam_ comes from _adamah_, indeed is _adamah_ made self-aware. To remove the barrier between _adam_ and _adamah_ is to stand in direct contact with the Ground of one's being. Moses does this fully, Joshua only halfway. Joshua is not yet Moses, and his angel does not push him further than he can actually go.

Moses's encounter with the angel is even more suggestive. While shepherding the flocks of his father-in-law Jethro, "YHVH'S angel appeared to Moses in a fiery blaze amidst a thornbush" (Exodus 3:2). This angel has no shape, a hint, perhaps, that Moses need not be reminded that his vision is an inner journey. Once the angel has caught Moses's attention he is no longer part of the story, and God himself speaks directly to Moses, commanding him, "Do not come nearer! Take off the sandals from your feet, you are standing on holy ground" (Exodus 3:5).

Unlike Joshua, Moses has no moment of confusion; he knows he is dealing with an angel, and with God. The fleeting nature of his encounter with the angel suggests that Moses moved swiftly through world-centered soul awareness and directly into God-centered spirit. It is because Moses is fully engaged with the ultimate Ground that he is told to remove both sandals. And what does this God want with Moses once the barrier between them is removed? We find the answer in Exodus 3:10: "I will dispatch you to Pharaoh to take my people, Israel's children, out of Egypt."

In other words, the encounter with God is the call for liberation from the narrow places of enslavement. Moses's encounter with God has worldly political ramifications. This is not a minor point. Having moved out of ego-centered mind and through world-centered soul Moses knows that self and other are one, though not yet the One. His encounter with God does not result in a Jesus-like exclamation, "The Father and I are one" (John 10:30), but rather in a command to return to the world of I-Thou and liberate it from the narrowness of I-It symbolized by the oppression of Pharaoh.

• • •

But Moses is an exception; most men and women in the Bible perceive angels as physical appearances, as human beings. That rule is nowhere more clear than in the eighteenth chapter of the book of Genesis when God visits Abraham while "he sat by the door of his tent in the heat of the day" (Genesis 18:1).

According to rabbinic midrash this visit takes place after Abraham has circumcised himself, his son Ishmael, and all the males of his household. He and the rest of the men are in agony over the cutting of their foreskins and, according to rabbinic midrash, God says to his angels, "Come let us go and visit the sick and see to the welfare of Abraham."[1]

The Bible itself does not mention angels but speaks of "three men" who approach Abraham's tent. In the midrash spun from this Bible story we are told that these "men" are in fact the archangels Michael, Gabriel, and Raphael who accompanied God on his visit to Abraham. Here is the biblical version:

> YHVH appeared to him [Abraham] at the oak groves
> of Mamre, as he sat by the door of his tent in the heat
> of the day. He [Abraham] looked up and noticed three
> men standing near him. As soon as he saw them he ran
> from the tent door to meet them, and bowing to the
> ground he said, "Gentlemen, please do not pass by your
> servant, but let some water be brought to wash your
> feet, and rest underneath this tree. I will bring some
> bread to pacify your hunger before resuming your jour-
> ney—after all, you have come to your servant's place."
> They replied, "Do as you have said." (Genesis 18:1–5)

It is important to see that it is God who plans to visit Abraham, yet it is three men that actually appear to him (and clearly the Bible itself does not tell us they are angels). The confusion here is between God and these three men, hinting again at the ultimate unity of God, humankind, and the angelic.

It may be that the early rabbis were troubled by this confusion, and did not want those who heard the story to imagine that God took the form of humans (unlike the Christian writers, who understood God to be the Father, the Son, and the Holy Spirit). So in the rabbis' inter-pretation of Genesis 18:1–5 the men become angels, allowing God to avoid any anthropomorphism in this case. Here is the version from *Genesis Rabbah*:

> Abraham was talking with God when he saw three men approaching his camp. He said to God, "Please, Lord, excuse me while I tend to the needs of these travelers." The men were in fact angels—Michael, Gabriel, and Raphael—sent by God that Abraham might fulfill his desire to provide hospitality to travel-ers. Each of the angels had a mission: Raphael came to heal the wound of Abraham's recent circumcision; Michael came to announce Sarah's future pregnancy; and Gabriel came to destroy Sodom.
>
> Abraham ran to greet the "men," inviting them to eat, drink, and sit beneath the shade tree growing by the entrance to his tent. This was a special tree, revealing the character of anyone sitting beneath it. If the visitor was just, compassionate, and receptive to hearing of the true God, the tree would spread its branches protec-tively. If not, the branches would shift and provide the visitor with no shade. The tree spread its branches wide and all three men were given shelter from the sun.[2]

Two points must be made here. First, Abraham leaves God to be of service to these three travelers. Abraham does not know them to be angels, and thinks them to be men like himself. Yet he tells God to wait while he serves these men a meal. In Abraham's hierarchy of concern, God comes last. This is no small teaching, and it tells us that in the mind of the rabbis the true way to serve God is to serve humanity. Coupled with God's command to Moses to liberate the Israelites, it also suggests that all encounters with God result not in an absorption into the godhead but in a return to humanity to be of service to its needs. Once an individual has experienced higher levels of consciousness, he or she cannot help but see all beings as part of the One and thus feel called to love God as both self and other, I and Thou.

The second point is that even with the aid of his magic tree, Abraham is still unaware that his visitors are angels. That is to say the goodness that the angels embody is not different from that which human beings can embody. While we can assume that the branches of Abraham's magic tree will shade the angels, we must realize that in Abraham's mind this is what is to be expected *whenever* good human beings sit beneath his tree. Again, the angels are not superior to humans, but symbolic of human potential.

When the meal was finished, so the midrash goes, Michael announced the birth of Isaac and returned to heaven, while Raphael, who had come to heal Abraham's wound but found him in no need of healing, accompanied Gabriel to Sodom.[3]

Normally angels have the capacity to travel at the speed of light, but Raphael and Gabriel were in this case angels of mercy, and they hesitated to execute their work of destruction, hoping that Abraham might turn aside God's decree against Sodom. They stalled until evening, but since no reprieve was given, they assumed the fate of the city was sealed and arrived there in a flash.[4]

That evening the two angels entered Sodom and, in a replay of their encounter with Abraham, they found Lot, Abraham's nephew, who also urged them to lodge with him and partake of his hospitality. The Bible is clear however that where Abraham saw "men," Lot saw "angels" (Genesis 19:1). Why did Lot see these strangers for what they really were, while Abraham confused them with humans? One would assume that Abraham, being closer to God, would see things more clearly than Lot. Again this hints at our premise. Lot saw the angels as "other," different from himself, while Abraham saw them as human, similar to himself. Abraham saw the matter more clearly, for he understood the nature of these travelers to be not unlike his own.

While the Bible remains silent on the matter, the midrash says that Lot sought to defend the city and its inhabitants, arguing with the angels as his uncle Abraham had argued with God hours earlier. He, like Abraham, told the angels that there were righteous people in the city who did not deserve to die for the sins of their neighbors. The angels were moved by his argument and were about to petition God to rethink his plan, when the citizens of Sodom stormed Lot's house demanding that he turn his visitors over to them to be raped.

> At first the angels were persuaded by Lot's defense of Sodom, but when the men surrounded the house and demanded that Lot's visitors be surrendered to them, they turned a deaf ear to Lot. Raphael grasped the hands of Lot, his wife, and their unmarried daughters, while Gabriel pushed his little finger against the foundation stone of the city causing Sodom to collapse. As Raphael and Gabriel led the family out of the city, they warned against looking back. Despairing over the fate of her married daughters who remained with their husbands in the city, Lot's wife glanced back and was

immediately turned to a pillar of salt. From that day
on, cattle came to lick the salt, and by evening it was
gone. But each morning the pillar returned and with it
the cattle.[5]

Now what shall we make of these stories of angelic destruction in
the context of God who is *Ehyeh asher Ehyeh*, "I will be whatever I
will be" (Exodus 3:14), the unpredictable creative force that liberates
humanity from enslavement to narrow-mindedness? In Lot's case
the enslavement was to be comfortable even in a place of immorality.
Here creative liberation required massive destruction. What happens
to Lot's wife deepens the story's meaning.

We are used to perceive the fate of Lot's wife as a punishment,
but, taking our text as myth, it is really something quite different:
Against the express orders of the angels, she looks back on the crum-
bling city, fearing for the fate of her daughters. Is it a mother's love
that is being punished here? No. While our myth reminds us that
looking back prevents us from moving forward, the image of an eternal pillar of salt licked by cattle is not negative.

A salt or mineral lick is part of a healthy ecosystem, providing cattle, deer, and other animals with the nutrients they need to grow
healthy bones and muscles. Animals will travel for miles to ingest
these much-needed nutrients. Lot's wife has become a source of life
for the cattle who are themselves an almost universal symbol of
motherhood and fertility. In other words, God did not punish Lot's
wife for loving her daughters; he transformed her into a pillar of life,
thus allowing her to love and be of help to God's creation.

• • •

Another angel myth of a mother's love for her child can be found in the biblical story of Hagar, Sarah's Egyptian slave and Abraham's consort, found in the book of Genesis, chapters 16 and 21.

Sarah begins to doubt God's promise that she will bear a son. Taking matters into her own hands, Sarah gives her slave girl, Hagar, to Abraham, hoping that any child born to Hagar will belong also to Sarah. When Hagar becomes pregnant, however, Sarah becomes jealous and treats Hagar harshly. To escape her mistress, Hagar flees into the desert. She is found at an oasis by an angel of God who asks her why she is running away. The angel tells Hagar to return to Sarah, and assures her that she is to give birth to a boy who is to be named *Ishmael*, Man of God. The Bible goes on to say that Hagar then "called the Name of YHVH Who spoke to her, 'You are the God of Vision,' for she said, 'Could I have seen God here, and after seeing him survived?'" (Genesis 16:13).

We are dealing with myth rather than history. How do we know? The Bible itself tells us something deeper than history is afoot. The angel says to the clearly pregnant Hagar, "You are pregnant and shall give birth to a son" (Genesis 16:11).

Why tell Hagar she is pregnant when that is so evident? The myth is pointing not to a biological birth but a psycho-spiritual one. This second conception is not physical but metaphorical: Hagar is to give birth to a level of awareness that realizes the unity of the human and the divine—Ishmael, literally *Ish*/man *m'*/from *El*/God. Whether or not we take Ishmael to be a historical figure, we can see the myth as saying something important about Hagar. She is the vessel from which a child of God will emerge—Hagar, here symbolizing all humans, carries within herself a level of consciousness that is fully in tune with the divine. The angel tells her this because it is the role of the angelic to point the human toward God and the greater unity in which all life resides.

Hagar returns to Abraham and Sarah's camp, gives birth, and raises her son Ishmael. In time, within a year of the destruction of Sodom, Sarah, too, gives birth to a son, Isaac.

The birth of Isaac does nothing to lessen Sarah's jealousy toward Hagar and Ishmael. While the majority of English translations of the Hebrew Bible seek to excuse Sarah's jealousy by telling us that Sarah saw Ishmael "mocking" Isaac, the Hebrew itself says only that Ishmael was "playing" with his younger half brother (Genesis 21:9). Again Sarah seeks to remove Hagar, this time along with her son, in this way ensuring that Isaac and not Ishmael will inherit Abraham's fortune and the mantle of leadership.

Sarah goes to her husband and demands that he "drive out this slave woman and her son" (Genesis 21:10). Not wishing to see any harm come to either Hagar or Ishmael, Abraham seeks counsel with God, and God urges him to follow the advice of Sarah, promising that he will see to the welfare of Abraham's firstborn. "So Abraham awoke early in the morning, took bread and a skin of water, and gave them to Hagar. He placed them on her shoulder along with the boy, and sent her off. She departed, and wandered about in the desert of Beer-sheba" (Genesis 21:14).

While the image of Abraham lifting Ishmael onto Hagar's shoulder may be touching, it is, given the time frame of the story itself, a bit absurd. Ishmael is a teenager at this point, far too big to be carried by his mother. The ancient rabbis noticed this discrepancy and derived yet another midrash from it. Sarah, they taught, had cast an evil spell on Ishmael as he was about to be expelled from the camp. The evil spell cast by Sarah made the boy sick and feverish, so that

Hagar had to carry him, grown-up as he was. In his fever he quickly drank all the water that Abraham had given them. It soon became obvious to Hagar that they would die in the desert, and she placed her son under a willow shrub and walked a ways off so as not to see him suffer.[6]

While the Bible tells us nothing of Sarah and her spells, both the biblical authors and the rabbis agree that it is when Hagar walks away from Ishmael that an angel of God calls to her (Genesis 21:17–19) saying, "Hagar, why are you distressed? God has heard your son's cry and will protect you both." God then opens Hagar's eyes and she perceives what she hadn't noticed before—a well of fresh water! Hagar fills the skin with water and helps her son to drink.

Importantly, it is not the angel that opens Hagar's eyes, but God. Again, the fluid passing from human to angel to God is the way this mythic tale hints at the greater unity of the human, the angelic, and the divine.

We notice, too, that the Bible does not say God creates the well for Hagar, but only that God opens Hagar's eyes that she might see what she had not seen before. This is what happens to humans when they move from ego-centered consciousness toward divine consciousness: our eyes are opened and we see what has been there all along, but which the ego-centered mind could not see.

• • •

One of the most famous angelic encounters found in the Hebrew Bible is Jacob's wrestling with the angel.

Jacob has left his father-in-law, Laban, and is making his way home along with his wives, children, servants, and herds. Hearing that his brother, Esau, is coming toward him at the head of four hundred warriors, Jacob assumes his brother plans to carry out his threat to murder him. Jacob seeks to protect his family by taking them across the river ford, and then to confront his brother alone. The Bible says, Jacob "got up that night and took his two wives, his two handmaids, and his eleven sons and crossed the ford of the Jabbok. When he had taken them across he sent for his possessions to follow them" (Genesis 32:22–23). He then recrosses the ford to face his brother.

> And Jacob was alone when a man wrestled with him until dawn. Seeing he could not defeat him, he wrenched Jacob's hip, pulling it from its socket. Then he said, "Release me, for the day is dawning." But Jacob said, "I will not release you unless you bless me." He said, "What is your name?" and he answered, "Jacob." He said, "Your name will no longer be Jacob, but *Yisra-El* [Israel], since you have wrestled with God and with men and have prevailed." Then Jacob said to him, "Now, please tell me your name." He answered, "Why should you be asking for my name?" and he blessed him there. Jacob named the place *Peniel* [Face of God] saying, "I have seen God face to face and yet my life continues." (Genesis 32:24–30)

The parallels of this story with the first Hagar story (Genesis 16) are striking. Both Hagar and Jacob are alone in the wilderness. Both are certain that they will shortly die. Both have encounters with beings greater than human. Both are moved to name either the being (in Hagar's case) or the place in which the being is encountered (in Jacob's case), and both use the verb "to see" in doing so. And both ultimately recognize that the "angel" and the "man" are both God.

Once more these myths are telling us that humanity, the angelic, and God are One, and there are some mortals among us with the capacity to see through the most narrow manifestation of Being, the human form, to the most inclusive manifestation, the divine form.

A rabbinic midrash regarding Jacob's wrestling with God makes this clear:

> As Jacob prepared to take his wives, consorts, children, and possessions across Jabbok's ford he noticed a shepherd seeking to cross with his sheep and camels. The shepherd approached Jacob proposing that each help the other in their quest to cross the ford. Jacob agreed so long as his family and possessions crossed to safety first. The shepherd agreed saying that he would transport Jacob's things and then Jacob would bring the shepherd's flocks and herds.
>
> Jacob nodded in agreement, and no sooner had he done so that all of his possessions suddenly appeared on the far side of the ford. Jacob then set about to take the shepherd's camels and sheep across. The crossing itself was easy, but no matter how many sheep and camels Jacob led across, when he returned to the other side still more awaited him. He persisted in this trial all night before finally losing patience.
>
> Jacob, thinking his tormentor was a wizard, suddenly leaped at the shepherd and strangled him crying, "Sorcerer!"

The shepherd laughed and said, "You think me a wizard. Let me show you with whom you are wrestling." The shepherd then touched his finger to the earth and the ground beneath the two of them burst into flame.

"You seek to defeat me with fire?" Jacob screamed, still choking the man. "I am made of fire!"[7]

Before we continue with this midrash, we must briefly explore Jacob's notion that he is made of fire. The Hebrew word for "man," *ish*, is comprised of three letters: *aleph*, *yod*, and *shin*. The Hebrew word for "fire," *esh*, contains two letters: *aleph* and *shin*. The word "fire" is thus incorporated into the word "man." The additional letter *yod* is one of the letters of God's Name, *Yod-Hey-Vav-Hey*, or YHVH. Hence a man is a holy fire, a fire who burns with the passion for truth and justice that is at the heart of God. The Hebrew word for "woman," *isha*, also contains the word *esh*, fire, followed by the letter *hey*, the second and fourth letters of God's Name. Thus woman is no less holy or fiery than man.

What does it mean that humans are holy fires? Fire both comforts and consumes. It can be used for good or evil. The same is true of people. We are consuming beings whose consumption can decimate a place and an entire planet if not held in check. Our consumption must be in the service of life and peace, and only then is it holy.

But who is this mysterious shepherd? The rabbis take him to be the archangel Michael, a master of fire, but *not* himself fire. Not realizing the true nature of humanity as holy fire, the angel Michael expects his fire magic to impress Jacob. But this is like a wave seeking to impress the ocean. The midrash continues:

Failing in his efforts to defeat Jacob, Michael called upon the host of angels under his command and was about to mortally wound Jacob when God Himself appeared and sapped His angels of their power.

God said to Michael, "Why are you seeking to harm Jacob who is My priest?" To which Michael replied, "Not so! I am Your priest and this one is a pretender. Only the unblemished can serve You as priest, and the wound I caused him disqualifies him."

God replied, "Michael, you are My priest in heaven, and Jacob is My priest on earth. Restore him!"

Michael then called to Raphael, the Angel of Healing. "Raphael, my friend, help me out of my distress! Cure this Jacob!"

And God said, "Now that you have restored him, tell Me why you sought to harm him?"

"I sought only to honor You."

"Then," God said, "I will give you that opportunity for you shall guard Jacob and the people that shall come forth from him until the end of time."

Then Michael turned to Jacob and said, "How is it that one who fears not angels stands in dread of his brother, Esau?"

All this time Jacob never once let go of Michael's throat. As day dawned, Michael said to Jacob, "Now let me go, the day breaks."

"And how is it that an archangel fears the daylight like a thief or a gambler?" Jacob said.

Then many angels appeared each calling to Michael,

"Come, Michael, dawn breaks and you must lead the choir in song. Without you we cannot sing!"

Fearing what might happen if the morning songs fell silent, Michael pleaded with Jacob to let him go. Unmoved, Jacob demanded a blessing from Michael before he would release him.

"What? Is the servant to bless the master? You heard what was said, I am to serve you and your descendants, how can I bless you?"

Still Jacob held on. So Michael said, "I was not empowered to bless you, but I will tell you a secret and if God blames me for doing so you must come to my defense. A time will come when God will change your name from Jacob to Israel, for you have wrestled with men and gods and have survived."[8]

This rabbinic version of the biblical tale not only embellishes the original, it solves a puzzle in the text itself. In the Bible Jacob's name is changed to Israel twice: once by the angel at the ford of the Jabbok (Genesis 32:29), and again by God a short time later (Genesis 35:10). Rather than imagine that God did not know about the first name change, the rabbis rework the story so that the angel is not actually changing Jacob's name but foretelling that God will do so later.

What are we to make of this midrash? The key is in the explanation the archangel Michael gives for wanting to kill Jacob. Michael claims that Jacob cannot serve God as a priest because he is wounded, a wound that Michael himself inflicted. This is no explanation at all since Michael sought to kill Jacob before injuring him. What really troubles the angel is that he suspects the human is usurping the angelic role. From the point of view of our metaphoric reading of angels, the myth is saying that the ego-centered mind cannot do without the angelic capacity, nor can the angelic do without the human.

"Michael, you are My priest in heaven" means that the angelic faculty is the way the human can move out of the slavery of ego-centered mind and toward the liberation of God-centered spirit. "And Jacob is My priest on earth" means that the human is the way the wisdom revealed by the angelic faculty, the wisdom of the I-Thou and I-I, is brought to bear on the events of the ego-centered world.

Yet if this so, if the two are somehow equal, why does God order Michael, and by extension all angels, to serve Jacob and humanity? The rabbis are reflecting the same insight revealed in the Bible, namely, that the circle of seeing begins with the human and ends with the human. The point is not simply to see beyond the human, but to look through the angelic and divine lenses of knowing back at the human so as to reveal humankind for what it is—a microcosm of the divine, the image and likeness of God (Genesis 1:26).

According to both the myths of the Bible and midrash, despite the healing efforts of Raphael, Jacob's wound could not be healed. The Bible tells us that Jacob limped because of his wound. Raphael kept the wound from being fatal, but not from being a constant reminder of Jacob's encounter with Michael. But there is more to this wound than a painful reminder of wrestling with an angel. Angels cannot be wounded. Woundedness is unique to humans, and in that woundedness may be a key to human spiritual maturation.

Jacob is called Jacob (*Ya'acov*) because he was born grasping the heel (*ah-cave*) of his brother, Esau. Jacob spent much of his life grasping: first his brother's birthright (Genesis 25:29–34), then his father's blessing (Genesis 27:1–37), then the daughters of Laban, then the sheep of Laban, and finally the blessing of the angel. Then as now, receiving a new name is symbolic of beginning a new life. The angel is telling Jacob that his life of grasping has come to an end. He is no longer the Heel-Clinger but *Yisra-El*, the God-Wrestler.

This is of crucial importance. Israel is not only Jacob's name but the name of the people that come after him, the people that the angel Michael is to serve. What does it mean to be Israel? It means one is a wounded warrior, one who, the Bible tells us, walks not at the pace of the warrior but at the pace of the nurturer, "a slow pace"—matching those of the cattle and the children (Genesis 33:13–14).

Israel the God-Wrestler walks at the pace of the toddler, the calf, and the nursing mother. Israel, unlike the earlier Jacob whose life was all about accumulating wealth and power, often by means of stealth and magic, is concerned with the weak, not the mighty. The trickster has become the nurturer. To borrow intentionally from the Gospels, Jacob who would be first is now Israel, who chooses to be last (Matthew 19:30); Jacob who was concerned only with himself is now Israel, whose passion is for the least of those among whom he dwells (Matthew 25:45).

This story adds greatly to our understanding of what it is to be transformed by God. We are not made to be more, but to be less. We are not to "play god" and lord it over others, but to be God, the God of compassion in the immediacy of our humanity. This is why Michael must serve Israel, the awakened human soul, and *not* Jacob, the unseeing ego-centered mind. Like the opening of Hagar's eyes that she might see the human world in a new way and drink from the well to which she had been blind, Israel is to be in the world in a new way and provide milk to the children and calves.

Israel in this case refers to anyone who has wrestled with the angelic and the divine—anyone who is attempting to integrate the ego-centered mind with the world-centered soul, and then to integrate both of these with the still greater and more inclusive God-centered spirit.

This transformation can only happen when we, like Jacob, *overcome* our aloneness, our alienation. In other words, the fundamental aspect of our consciousness that we must overcome is the illusory notion of the narrow mind that each of us is all alone—separate and alienated from God and everyone and everything else. This sense of alienation is the original error of humanity, and the angelic potential helps us to overcome it. To understand this feeling of alienation more clearly, we need to look at the underlying myth.

• • •

We find the original myth of alienation in the Bible in a story so well known that its familiarity might hinder our understanding: When God discovers that Adam has eaten from the Tree of Knowledge of Good and Evil, God says, "Behold the man has become *achad mimenu*, knowing good and evil. Now he might reach out and take also from the Tree of Life, and eat it and gain immortality!' So YHVH God banished him from the Garden of Eden, to work the soil from which he was taken. And having driven out the man, He stationed at the east of the Garden of Eden the cherubim and the flame of the ever-turning sword, to guard the way to the Tree of Life" (Genesis 3:22–24).

To understand this myth we have to understand the Hebrew

phrase *achad mimenu*, usually translated as "like one among us." The Hebrew, however, literally means "unique from us," or "one separate from us." Eating from the tree does not make Adam like God, as the serpent promised (Genesis 3:5); rather he becomes alienated from God, first psychologically and then physically. Becoming *achad* means that humanity can no longer see itself as a part of the divine whole. Instead, humanity imagines itself to be apart from both God and nature—a separate volitional force, an ego-centered mind only.

Most of us suffer from this notion that we are somehow other than the whole. The truth is so very different. There is no "I" separate from the Whole, and that feeling of separation is simply an experience of *maya*, the Sanskrit word for illusion. Mythical angelic encounters often push the ego-centered mind to realize the greater Whole in which it rests (and this is the purpose of angelic encounters in the first place). It is the ego-centered mind that meets the angelic, thereby offering the I-It level of human consciousness the opportunity to open to the truth of I-Thou and perhaps even I-I.

The God-centered spirit of I-I does not negate the ego-centered mind of I-It, but it places it in the larger Whole in which all things exist. Our myths of angelic encounters do not entail the negation of the human who meets the angel. It is not that we, in our human-angelic encounters, forget our names, homes, and belongings, but that we realize that we are so much more than the self that is defined by the material.

In the Eden story, God is going to expel Adam from the Garden not simply because God fears Adam could eat from the Tree of Life and thereby gain immortality (God had actually never prohibited the first couple from eating of the Tree of Life or any other tree in the Garden, *except* for the Tree of Knowledge of Good and Evil), but that by eating from it without first overcoming this state of *achad*, alienation, Adam would be eternally cut off from God, from Adam's highest and most inclusive self; he would be forever locked in a world of seeming separation and duality. Thus the expulsion from the Garden is not so much a punishment as it is a preventive.

With this deeper reading of the story of the Expulsion from Eden we can also take a fresh look at the role of the cherubim in this myth: "[God] stationed at the east of the Garden of Eden the cherubim and the flame of the ever-turning sword, to guard the way to the Tree of Life" (Genesis 3:24).

We assume that the cherubim are violent figures who will use their flaming sword to keep Adam from returning to the Garden and eating from the Tree of Life. Yet the only other time we learn about cherubim is in Exodus where God commands Moses to place two carved cherubim on the cover of the Ark (Exodus 25:18) and tells Moses, "I will talk with you from above the Cover, from the space between the two cherubim that are on the Ark of the Covenant" (Exodus 25:22). The cherubim are in fact symbols of God's presence.

There are two ways to understand this notion of guarding "the way to the Tree of Life." Either the cherubim are there to protect the Tree from any invasion Adam might think to mount, or they are there to safeguard the way to the Tree when and if Adam, i.e., humanity, is ready to return and take the next step on the journey of human spiritual evolution. In our understanding the second is the more accurate reading.

This very first meeting of humans and angels in the Bible reveals them to be protectors of our way home. If we follow the light of the flaming sword we will find the angelic power protecting the path we must walk. What is true of this first meeting is true of subsequent meetings as well. Angels—our angelic potential—can take us out of the alienated and narrow ego-centered mind and reveal a more inclusive consciousness that is our great awakening. And the angels who are at the forefront of leading us toward this awakening are the archangels.

Four

The Archangels

THE WORD "ARCHANGEL," comes from the Greek *archangelos*, which is made up of two words, *arch*, meaning "first," "primary," or "chief," and *angelos*, "messenger." Among other angels, we are introduced to three of the archangels in the following midrash:

> When God prepared to create humankind, He summoned His angels to Him to take counsel. They were not of one mind. The Angel of Love applauded the idea, saying that these new beings would know true love and affection. The Angel of Truth, however, thought little of the idea, arguing that humanity would become masters of the lie. The Angel of Justice sided with Love and argued that humanity would practice

justice. But the Angel of Peace stood with Truth and warned that the way of humanity was war.

God was not happy with the opposing arguments and to make plain His displeasure, He tossed the Angel of Truth down from heaven to the earth. Such contempt outraged the other angels and they complained loudly. God replied, "Truth will spring back out of the earth" (*Genesis Rabbah* 8:5).[1]

God then summoned the archangel Michael and his band and inquired of them as to the creation of humanity. Michael and his band opposed the creation saying, "What is humanity, that You remember them?" (Psalm 8:4). God was angry with this challenge, and, stretching forth His little finger, consumed all of Michael's angels in a great blaze, leaving only Michael remaining. The same fate befell the angels of archangel Gabriel when they too raised the same objection.

A third band of angels was summoned before God, these led by the archangel Labbiel. Hearing of the fate of the prior bands, Labbiel spoke to his angels saying, "We have heard of the fate of those who challenge God's decision, therefore let us not suffer similarly. When asked regarding the creation of the human say not, "What is humanity, that You remember them?" but rather, "Lord of the Universe, it is well that You consider such a creation. Create humanity according to Your will, and we will attend to them, and reveal to them all our secrets."

Well pleased, God changed Labbiel's name to Raphael which means Rescuer and Healer, for he had rescued the angels from the wrath of God, and God placed into his safekeeping all the cures used in heaven and earth.[2]

Labbiel/Raphael reinforces our understanding of the role of angels in human life. They safeguard the ego-centered mind even as they reveal the cure for the state of *achad* that maintains the illusion of separation between us humans and the divine Whole. But what are we to make of the other angels in this midrash who oppose the creation of humanity?

Not every encounter with the angelic faculty is a positive one. There is a dark side to the angelic consciousness, one that leads us even further into the delusion of separation. How is this possible? If the ego-centered mind is strong enough it can pervert the inkling of what the angels have to offer and read their message not as an invitation to transcend the self but to deify it—not to move toward God, but to insist that the self is God.

Archangels have a unique significance in bringing us the divine message. Their names are difficult to determine since the archangel traditions found in Judaism, Christianity, and Islam provide us with multiple and conflicting lists of names. Indeed, when all the lists are compared we find a total of thirty angels competing to be named as one of the seven archangels. There is no way to agree which of these are the "true" archangels. Most likely there is no definite list of archangels at all. Rather, there might be a general sense of an angelic hierarchy that isn't all that concerned with names.

The need for a hierarchy stems from the explosion of angels in the minds and tales of the Jewish and Christian sages. According to the ancient rabbis, there is not a blade of grass on earth that lacks its protecting angel in heaven.[3] And St. Augustine wrote, "every visible thing in this world is put under the charge of an angel."[4] Angels are everywhere, but some are especially important to humankind.

The canonical books of the Hebrew Bible do not present the concept of archangels at all, and the angels that are mentioned are not named—except for Michael and Gabriel in the book of Daniel. The names given to the angels come from rabbinic midrash and are, according to Rabbi Simeon ben Lakish of Tiberias (230–270 CE), influenced by the names of Zoroastrian angels about whom the Jews learned during their captivity in Babylonia in the sixth century BCE. This is why, Rabbi Simeon said, in the book of Daniel, which deals with events that took place during that captivity, the angels carry names unknown to previous Jewish writers.

The New Testament book of Revelation, written by John of Patmos at the close of the first century CE, makes multiple mention of seven angels but does not call them archangels (Revelation 8:2; 15:1–8; 16:1; 17:1; 21:9). Archangels are mentioned twice in the New Testament, but only one such angel is named: in Jude 9 the angel Michael is identified as an archangel in dispute with the devil. In 1 Thessalonians 4:16 we are told that the return of Jesus to earth will happen "with a cry of command, with the archangel's call and with the sound of God's trumpet," and Christian tradition assumes that the archangel mentioned here refers to Michael as well.

The *Book of Tobit*, a second-century BCE text that is part of the literary collection called the *Apocrypha*, from the Greek meaning "those having been hidden away," is the first to introduce us to the angel Raphael who says (*Tobit* 12:15) that he is one of the seven angels who stand before the divine glory, ever ready to do the bidding of God. The Apocrypha are Jewish texts of uncertain authorship. Their authenticity is questioned by both Jewish and Protestant authorities, and they are excluded from the Bibles of these two faiths. The Catholic and Orthodox canons on the other hand include these texts and consider them holy and divinely inspired.

Another apocryphal text, *2 Esdras*, refers to two additional angels, Uriel and Jeremiel, and labels the latter an archangel as well.

The rabbinic midrashim identify seven archangels, though they do not agree as to their names. There is consensus that Michael, Raphael, and Gabriel are archangels, but the sages differ as to who the other four archangels are, with different rabbis backing one or another of the following named angels: Uriel, Sariel, Raguel, Remiel, Zadiel, Jophiel, Haniel, and Chamiel. The rabbis may have been inspired by the apocryphal *Book of Enoch* where seven archangels are identified: Michael, Gabriel, Raphael, Uriel, Raguel, Seraqael, and Haniel.

Islam, in its Aqidah, the Six Articles of Belief derived from the Hadith, the sayings and deeds of Muhammad, include a belief in angels along with belief in Allah, the Prophets, the Books, the Day of Judgment, and Destiny. While Islam recognizes many named angels, four are designated as archangels: Jibril (Gabriel), who dictated the Qur'an to the prophet Muhammad; Mika'il (Michael), the archangel of mercy; Israfil (Raphael), who will blow the trumpet on Judgment Day; and 'Izra'il (Azrael), the angel of death.

Fortunately, given the number of angels contending for the rank of archangel, our concern is with the potential of angels rather than their individual status, and thus we will focus on the following four archangels: Michael/Mika'il, Gabriel/Jibril, Raphael/Israfil—since Judaism, Christianity, and Islam agree on these three—and Uriel, because Judaism and Christianity both name him as an archangel. In a later chapter on the angel of death we will look at the fourth of Islam's archangels, 'Izra'il, and comparable angels in Judaism and Christianity.

Here is a midrash introducing us to the four archangels (*Numbers Rabbah* 2:10): As the Holy One blessed be He created four winds (directions) and four banners (for Israel's army), so also did He make four angels to surround His Throne—Michael, Gabriel, Uriel, and Raphael. Michael is on its right, corresponding to the tribe of Reuben; Uriel on its left, corresponding to the tribe of Dan, which was located in the north; Gabriel in front, corresponding to the tribe of Judah as well as Moses and Aaron who were in the east; and Raphael in the rear, corresponding to the tribe of Ephraim which was in the west.

Michael

The Hebrew name Michael, *mi k'El*, means "Who is like God." Judaism and Christianity consider Michael the chief of the angels, though perhaps not the most powerful of all angels.

In Judaism Michael first appears as a named angel in the book of Daniel, alongside the angel Gabriel, to defeat the Persians (Daniel 10:13). As we have seen, Jewish tradition identifies him as the angel who announced to Sarah that she would give birth to a son (*Genesis Rabbah* 48:9–50:2). In addition he is said to have recorded the sale of Esau's birthright to Jacob (*Genesis Rabbah* 63:14), rescued Abraham from the fiery furnace (*Genesis Rabbah* 44:13), accompanied God to Mount Sinai (*Deuteronomy Rabbah* 2:34), instructed Moses (*Deuteronomy Rabbah* 11:10), was sent but failed to take Moses's soul at his death (*Ecclesiastes Rabbah* 9:11), stood by Moses's side after his death (*Deuteronomy Rabbah* 11:10), defeated the army of the Persian king (*Exodus Rabbah* 18:5), and aided the Jews of Persia when Haman sought their destruction (*Esther Rabbah* 7:12).

According to the rabbis Michael is made up entirely of snow while Gabriel is composed of fire. Whereas in the natural world fire and snow cannot coexist, in the divine realm they do (*Deuteronomy Rabbah* 5:12). The fact that both archangels appear together in so many stories, and that the rabbis place them together around God's throne, is meant to show that God reconciles all opposites in the nonduality of the I-I.

While often accompanied by Gabriel, Michael is thought to be his superior (Babylonian Talmud, tractate *Berakhot* 4b), and is identified with the *Shekhinah* or Holy Spirit (*Exodus Rabbah* 2:5).

The canonical book of Daniel that first introduces Michael is a mid-second-century BCE text that tells the story of an Israelite named Daniel who was taken captive and exiled to Babylonia in the sixth century BCE. There, according to the story, Daniel's intelligence gained him some fame, and he was trained as an advisor in the court of the king, a task at which he excelled.

Though true to his calling as a counselor to the king, Daniel maintained his identity as a Jew and a follower of the Jewish religion, a decision that made him vulnerable to attack by jealous rivals. His rivals convinced the king to issue an edict ordering a thirty-day suspension of all worship to any god but the king. Violators of the edict would be fed to the lions (Daniel 6:6–7).

Despite the edict Daniel continued his practice of praying to God three times each day. Daniel prayed in his house, in an upper room with windows facing toward Jerusalem. Those who conspired against him waited until Daniel was praying and then turned him over to the authorities.

The king was loath to cause any harm to Daniel, but was forced by his own edict to condemn his counselor to death. That evening

Daniel was sealed into a pit with lions. At dawn the next day the king raced to the pit to discover the fate of Daniel, and found him safe and well, for "God sent his angel and closed tight the lions' mouths so that they could not harm me" (Daniel 6:22).

As the story continues, Daniel is in the third week of a modified fast in which he abstained from "fine bread," meat, and wine (Daniel 10:3). He was standing on the bank of the Tigris River when he looked up (Daniel 10:5–6) and saw a man dressed in fine linen tightened at the waist with a golden belt. It seemed to Daniel that the man's body was chiseled like rock crystal, with legs and arms that gleamed like polished bronze. The man's face flashed like lightning, and his eyes danced like torch flames, and the sound of the man's voice sounded like a thunderous cheering crowd.

The "man" is really an angel, and while he remains nameless, he is probably the archangel Gabriel. The angel speaks to Daniel about fighting the Persians, and thereby mentions the archangel Michael: "I battled the Persians for twenty-one days and would have died had not Michael, one of the chief angels, come to my aid. He battled the Persian prince and I escaped" (Daniel 10:13). The man then says (Daniel 10:20–21) that he must return to battle the Persians and soon the Greeks as well, but that he was sent to tell Daniel what is written in the book of truth—that there is no one to defend against these enemies except Michael.

As in so many angelic encounters, Daniel sees the angel on the bank of the Tigris in the shape of a man, suggesting that the angel is a projection of Daniel's own inner potential. To make it clear that Daniel is having a psycho-spiritual encounter, a vision, he tells us that during the encounter he became physically weak and grew deathly pale (Daniel 10:8). Daniel is shifting from the normal waking state of ego-centered mind that is linked to the physical world of the body to a higher world-centered soul state that transcends the body. Then, when Daniel hears the sound of the angel's voice, he falls face first to the ground, lost in a trance (Daniel 10:9).

As Daniel lies on the ground (Daniel 10:10–12) the "man" walks over to him, touches him, and pulls him up to a kneeling position. The angel then orders Daniel to stand up so that the two of them can speak, presumably as equals. Here again is a hint that the human and the angelic are one. The angel tells Daniel not to fear, and explains that God has been watching over Daniel ever since he committed himself to the pursuit of wisdom. Daniel's words drew God's attention, and it is because of his words that the angel now stands before him. The angel is revealing two things to Daniel and through Daniel to us. First, that setting our minds to gain understanding initiates the process of angelic encounters, and second, that words can be a tool for invoking angelic consciousness. Angels are symbols of understanding and wisdom.

Daniel is overwhelmed by the conversation and protests that he, a mere mortal, cannot dare to talk with an angel. In fact, he confesses to the angel, the conversation has left him trembling, weak, and unable to catch his breath (Daniel 10:16–17). The angel revives Daniel and warns him that the Babylonians are only the first in a series of foreign powers that will threaten Israel. Yet Daniel need not despair of the future, because in the end the angel Michael, the guardian of the Jewish people, will rise up and deliver the people from their oppressors (Daniel 12:1).

Just when this time of redemption is to occur is not revealed to Daniel, nor does it matter with regard to our own interpretation. What does matter is that the archangel Michael is called the protector of Israel. As we have seen earlier, in the world of angelic archetypes *Israel* represents that state of human-divine unity granted to Jacob in his wrestling with the angel (Michael, according to the midrash) at Jabbok's Ford. In the book of Daniel, as in the midrashic retelling of Jacob's wrestling with the angel, we learn that when we achieve the status of Israel we will have access to the powers of Michael.

The book of Daniel reveals that Michael is our guardian angel, and he protects us by waking us up to the greater Whole we have been ignoring since leaving Eden under the false notion of *achad*, alienated ego-centered mind. Michael helps us shift from ego-centered mind to the broader awareness of world-centered soul.

One of the Dead Sea Scrolls, entitled *War of the Sons of Light Against the Sons of Darkness*, supports this understanding of Michael, referring to him as the "Prince of Light."

The Dead Sea Scrolls, consisting of approximately one thousand documents, were discovered in eleven caves in the Qumran region of the Judean desert. The first discovery in 1947 was accidental and made by a Bedouin sheepherder named Muhammad Ahmed ed-Hamed. The scrolls reflect the life of the Jewish community at Qumran sometime in the first half of the second century BCE. The Qumran Jews saw themselves as the elect of Israel who held to the true faith prescribed by God. The Qumran Jews believed that a coming war with the enemies of Israel would be divine and apocalyptic, and they themselves would be its victors.

The *War of the Sons of Light Against the Sons of Darkness* is their strategic manual for this coming battle. Written sometime in the late first century BCE or early first century CE, the text deals with the forty-year war that the remnant of the tribes of Israel, here called the

Sons of Light, will wage when they return from the "wilderness of the nations" and return to the "wilderness of Jerusalem." According to this manual, God will send an angelic army led by the angel Michael to fight alongside Israel (*War of the Sons of Light Against the Sons of Darkness*, chapter 14).

What is of interest here is not so much the angelic army, but the reference to two types of wilderness, that of the nations and that of Jerusalem. The "nations" refers to the countries and peoples among whom the Jews were exiled. Calling one's place of exile a "wilderness" is not surprising. But to also use the wilderness metaphor for the heart of one's homeland—Jerusalem, the City of Peace—suggests something else may be implied here.

The Hebrew word for "wilderness" is *midbar*, sharing the same root, *dvr*, as the Hebrew words for "word," "speech," and "thing." A wilderness can be both a desolate and silent terrain where things are few and far between, and a place filled with things and sounds and rife with overwhelming consumption, both material and intellectual. The scroll may be saying that the human challenge is to survive not only the wilderness of want, but also the wilderness of plenty.

Given our understanding of angels as mythic expressions of inner spiritual capabilities, we read this War Between Light and Dark as an inner conflict. It takes place only when we have exhausted the promise of things and sounds—words and ideas—and have nowhere else to turn but to the heart of the city itself. A wilderness of words surrounds the City of Peace, and this too must be passed through and left behind. Neither things nor ideas are enough to bring us peace. Only when both are discarded can we enter the city. And who guides us there? The archangel Michael, the Prince of Light.

Light doesn't defeat darkness; it dispels it. In the "wilderness of the nations" we are mostly under the spell of the thing. In the "wilderness of Jerusalem" we are much under the spell of the word. And the second is the greater spell—the word "spell" itself teaches us that. "To spell" is to break a word into its alphabetic parts. "To cast a spell" is to build up those parts into words that create psychic delusions. "Spell" is all about words. To be under a spell is to be lost in the illusion cast by words.

The great spell of the wilderness of Jerusalem, its great illusion, is that words can lead to truth. The great darkness of that wilderness is the realization that they often do not. The Sons of Darkness are the feelings of despair that overcome us when we realize there is no salvation in things or words. We are creatures of matter and intellect, and if neither can save us we cannot be saved—or so says the ego-centered mind.

This is the ultimate exhaustion of ego. And it is only when the ego is drained, when there is no breath left in the body, as Daniel puts it, that we are at last open to the presence of the angelic consciousness that dispels—or "dis-spells"—the darkness threatening the ego-centered mind. Michael simply appears. We cannot make him come. We cannot summon him. We can only reach the end of our options. When there is nothing left that we can do, when we have run out of idols to worship—then the angelic emerges.

The archetypal war between light and darkness finds its Christian expression in the book of Revelation. Here we meet the angel Michael in combat with the Great Dragon who symbolizes this darkness: "And war broke out in heaven; Michael and his angels fought against the dragon. The dragon and his angels fought back, but they were defeated, and there was no longer any place for them in heaven. The great dragon was thrown down, that ancient serpent,

who is called the Devil and Satan, the deceiver of the whole world—
he was thrown down to the earth, and his angels were thrown down
with him" (Revelation 12:7–9).

With the defeat of the dragon in heaven, the war now shifts to the
earth:

> So when the dragon saw that he had been thrown
> down to the earth, he pursued the woman who had
> given birth to the male child. But the woman was
> given the two wings of the great eagle, so that she
> could fly from the serpent into the wilderness, to her
> place where she is nourished for a time, and times, and
> half a time. Then from his mouth the serpent poured
> water like a river after the woman, to sweep her away
> with the flood. But the earth came to the help of the
> woman; it opened its mouth and swallowed the river
> that the dragon had poured from his mouth. Then the
> dragon was angry with the woman, and went off to
> make war on the rest of her children, those who keep
> the commandments of God and hold the testimony of
> Jesus. (Revelation 12:13–17)

While John is writing for Christians, the implication of his writing is far more universal. The Dragon is the Deceiver, the one who
spreads lies, illusions, and delusions, and the ultimate delusion is
the ego-centered mind's insistence that the "I" is like God, not in
the sense of the I-I nonduality, but in the false sense of I-It duality.
By casting the Dragon down to earth, into the human sphere, the
myth is telling us the dragon must be found and slain in our ego-
centered minds.

We may assume that John of Patmos was quite familiar with the older book of Daniel and the legend of the dragon that it contains. By reading how Daniel defeated the dragon in his day we can discover how best to slay it in ours.

In the Apocrypha we read that after Daniel had proven to the Babylonian king that his god Bel was a fraud perpetuated by the false god's priests, the king demanded that Daniel worship a dragon god instead. Daniel refused and claimed that he would slay the dragon without using weapons of any kind. The king accepted Daniel's challenge to test his dragon god, telling him that should he fail he would forfeit his life.

Daniel made cakes of boiled tar, animal fat, and hair, and fed them to the dragon, which promptly ate them (Daniel 14:27). The cakes exploded in the dragon's stomach and the beast burst open and died.

This is one way to slay the dragon of delusion: feed it to bursting. Applied to our inner dragon which demands that the I-It perspective of the ego-centered mind be worshipped as the sole reality, this myth suggests that if we are to free ourselves from the worship of the false god of self, we might need to develop greater openness and mindfulness—"feed ourselves with the world's knowledge"—until we can no longer maintain the illusion of *achad*, the separate, isolated, and alienated self.

• • •

Dragon slaying is a recurring theme in Christianity, and it is always linked to the archangel Michael. St. George, for example, a third-century CE Roman soldier from Anatolia, has become one of the most venerated saints in the Anglican Church and in Eastern Churches. Because his role as the dragon-slayer is reminiscent of the book of Revelation, St. George is thought by many to be the human incarnation of the archangel Michael.

According to legend a monstrous dragon ravaged a city in Libya and its surroundings. The dragon's breath carried plague, and the people fed the beast two sheep each day in the hopes of keeping it full. When this failed they resorted to offering the dragon a human victim chosen by lots.

It so happened that the king's daughter drew the fateful lot and was to be sacrificed to the dragon. While the king offered to pay handsomely for a substitute, the people had agreed in advance that no substitutions would be allowed, regardless of who requested them. Just as the young woman, dressed in a bridal gown, was being led to her death, St. George rode by.

The woman urged him to ride on, but St. George refused, and when the dragon appeared St. George attacked it. Using his lance like a hypnotist would use a pendulum, St. George put the dragon into a trance. He asked the woman for her girdle, which he tied tightly around the dragon's neck, thus making it impossible for the beast to breathe deeply enough to spit fire and fight back. Then St. George handed the other end of the girdle to the princess, who could now lead the dragon around as one might walk a dog. The three of them returned to the city where St. George converted the people to Christianity, then slew the dragon by cutting off its head. The king offered the good knight half his kingdom, but not the hand of his daughter in marriage. St. George declined and departed.

What are we to make of this story? Because of the possible link between the archangel Michael and St. George, and remembering that Michael threw the dragon down to earth where St. George killed it, we suggest this interpretation: the dragon is the insatiable craving of ego-centered consciousness. At first we think we can placate the dragon with offerings of food, but we soon discover that the only thing it wants to devour is humanity itself. In order to survive, the dragon must eat the human.

Here the human is symbolized by the bride. She represents the human half of a human-divine union. Israel, the Jewish people, for example, sees itself as the Bride of God, and the Church speaks of itself as the Bride of Christ. The bride seeks out her husband and desires union with him. The dragon interferes by desiring to eat her. In other words, the dragon symbolizes that which keeps humanity from realizing (with the aid of angelic consciousness) its greater unity with God.

St. George, the human expression of the archangel Michael, is that aspect of angelic consciousness that first controls and then slays the powerful illusion of *achad*.

Thus it is the king's daughter, and not St. George, who leads the dragon about on a leash. Angelic consciousness tames the beast, and then places it in the hands of the ego-centered mind, suggesting that the ego is not evil in and of itself, but in the grips of evil as long as it allows the dragon to dominate it.

In the Middle Ages the archangel Michael became very popular among Christians, eventually giving rise to his own cult. From Mont Saint Michel in France to the Monte Sant'Angelo in Italy, many churches and chapels were named after the archangel. His feast day, called Michaelmas, was (but is no longer) an obligatory holy day. Today Michaelmas is called the Feast of Saints Michael, Gabriel, and Raphael, and is celebrated on September 29. Its close relation with the autumnal equinox and the coming days of darkness suggests that Michael, as the central warrior angel, battles against the forces of darkness, and is thus the perfect angel upon whom to call as winter approaches.

The cult of Michael grew so large over the centuries that modern scholars have been suspecting that more than just angel worship had been at work. There are several theories, but many scholars link the popularity of Michael to the ancient god Mithra and the end of the religion of Mithraism under the evolving Church.

Mithra was the pre-Zoroastrian sun god of ancient Persia who became very popular in the Roman Empire during the early centuries of the common era. By the third century CE Mithraism was officially recognized as one of the religions of Rome, and temples devoted to his worship were found throughout the empire. With the conversion of Emperor Constantine and the transformation of the polytheistic Roman Empire into the monotheistic and exclusively Christian Roman Empire, Mirthraism was outlawed, and those who followed the faith were forced to convert to Christianity.

As is common with forced conversions, the followers of Mithra found ways to integrate their original faith into their new one. In this case the legends of Mithra as a warrior god and the adoption of Mithraism as a faith for many Roman soldiers may have led his followers to elevate the archangel Michael, the archangel in charge of God's armies, to the status of a disguised Mithra. This would explain why so many former temples dedicated to Mithra over time became churches dedicated to the archangel Michael, and why Michael is even today the patron saint of warriors.

Concerned by the large number of "Michael worshippers," Pope Zachary officially "demoted" Michael, along with Raphael and Uriel, from archangels to saints in the year 745. Nevertheless, the angelic status of these newly minted saints was never lost to the common people, as is evident in the much later Prayer to Saint Michael, Archangel, added to the Catholic liturgy by Pope Leo XIII in 1886: "Saint Michael, Archangel, defend us in battle. Be our defense against the wickedness and snares of the devil. May God rebuke him, we humbly pray. And you, Prince of the heavenly host, by the power of God, thrust into Hell Satan and the other evil spirits who prowl the world for the ruin of souls. Amen."

In Islam, the archangel Mika'il is mentioned only once in the Qur'an, in the second and longest Sura called *Al Baqarah*, "The Cow" (because it contains a story about Moses and the Israelites debating over the sacrifice of a cow). Unlike Jewish and Christian traditions that place Michael above Gabriel, Islam always sees him as inferior to the higher ranked Jibril. Also unlike the Christian understanding of Michael as a warrior, Mika'il is the archangel of mercy who brings rain to the earth, a precious commodity in the desert lands from which Islam came, and who bestows material blessings on the righteous in this life.

Gabriel

If Michael is the power that slays dragons of the mind and frees us from the idolatry of things and words, the archangel Gabriel (Jibril in Islam) is the power that illuminates the next step in human awakening: transformation from ego-centered mind to world-centered soul.

The Hebrew name Gabriel, *gav-ri-El*, or "God's Strength," is derived from two Hebrew words, *gever*, man, and *El*, God. Gabriel is the angelic faculty that points the human in the direction of the divine. Gabriel calls us to transformation, and is often depicted carrying a trumpet to get our attention that we might heed the divine call. Hence it is not surprising to find Gabriel as the angel of annunciation, death, resurrection, and revelation, for each of these has transformation at its core.

Gabriel appears four times in the Bible, twice in the book of Daniel and twice in the Gospel according to Luke. In Daniel 8:16–26, the first time he is mentioned in the Bible, Gabriel interprets one of Daniel's visions. In Daniel 9:21–27 he comes to bring the prophet "wisdom and understanding." In Luke he foretells the births of John and Jesus (Luke 1:19 and Luke 1:26).

Right before Gabriel's first biblical appearance, the prophet Daniel has a vision that surpasses his understanding (Daniel 8:1–15). The angel Gabriel then appears to Daniel in human form to help clarify this vision for him (Daniel 8:16). Daniel sees himself standing by the river Ulai in Susa, the capital of Persia. He looks up and sees a two-horned ram, with one horn longer than the other, charging wildly to the west, north, and south. Nothing can withstand its attacks, and its strength grows. A male goat then appears out of the west, with a single horn in the center of its forehead. This goat savagely races toward the ram, moving so fast that its hooves seem not to touch the ground. The goat tramples the ram, breaking both its horns, and killing it. The goat then grows ever stronger, but at the height of its power it breaks its single horn and four horns take its place. From one of these comes a fifth horn, and this one, small at first, grows to an extraordinary size reaching from earth to the host of heaven where it throws down to earth both angels and stars and tramples them. The goat challenges the prince of the host, toppling the burnt offering he was bringing to God, and destroying the heavenly sanctuary. Daniel then hears a voice crying out, "How long will the offering and the sanctuary lay fallen?" A second voice answers saying, "The sanctuary will be restored after twenty-three hundred days."

Daniel is confused by what he has seen and heard in his vision. Suddenly a man appears before him and he hears a human-sounding voice calling to the man saying, "Gabriel, explain this vision to him." Daniel prostrates himself before the man, whom he now knows to be the angel Gabriel. Gabriel says, "Know this: this vision is for the end-time." As the angel Gabriel speaks Daniel falls into a trance, his face pressed to the ground, and remains in this state until the angel touches him and raises him to his feet.

The ram, like the dragon, represents chaos. It runs round and round and nothing can escape it or stop it. It grows in strength but not discernment. Its two horns represent the dualism that is the hallmark of the ego-centered I-It view of things.

Opposing this ram is the male goat from the west. Why the west? When Adam and Eve leave the Garden of Eden they travel eastward, the one direction not mentioned by Daniel regarding his rampaging ram. "East" is symbolic of the alienation from the Garden and the wholeness the Garden represents. The ram of chaos is as east of Eden as one can get. The goat from the west is coming from the direction of Eden. This goat has a single horn growing between its eyes, symbolizing a more singular vision, like the I-Thou, the "We" of the world-centered soul.

The single-horned goat slays the dual-horned ram, and grows strong by destroying it. But the death of the ego-centered mind is not yet true awakening. True awakening is realizing that the ego-centered mind *and* the world-centered soul are each legitimate expressions of the God-centered spirit, the I-I that embraces both the I-It and the I-Thou.

Because the goat is not yet fully God-realized, it slays the ram. The slaying of the ego-centered mind does not lead to peace and tranquility, but to further chaos, for now the goat has no means to function on the plane of seemingly separate things. The goat is plunged into a wild state in which its single horn, its symbol of unity and unified direction and purpose, is broken, and four horns appear in its place.

The single horn represents unity without diversity, the four horns represent diversity without unity. The fifth horn that emerges from the four represents a false unity to which humanity can fall prey. This is the unity of totalitarianism and conformity that eliminates all diversity in favor of a lifeless homogeneity. This is not the nonduality of God-centered spirit. This imposed rather than organic unity tramples down the divine order that embraces both the one and the many in a greater nonduality, topples truth from its place, and does more damage than even the rampaging two-horned ram with which Daniel's vision opened.

By interpreting Daniel's vision, Gabriel is the announcer, the fore-teller, the pointer of the way. He is telling us that we cannot go quietly from ego-centered mind to world-centered soul, and from world-centered soul to God-centered spirit. The transition from one state to the other is not smooth but chaotic. Yet we need not despair: by working through the stages we will eventually achieve the fullest level of awareness.

Gabriel's role in all of this is quite different from that of Michael. As we saw, Michael was an active player in subduing the dragon of chaos. Gabriel is the giver of wisdom and insight; he explains what is happening but is not an active participant in that happening.

The book of Daniel makes this explicit in its second appearance of the archangel Gabriel. Daniel relates that during his time of afternoon prayer when he was confessing and making supplication to

God, "the man Gabriel" descended from the sky "in swift flight" to speak with him. Daniel recognizes Gabriel from his earlier vision, and the "man" addresses Daniel by name, saying that he has now "come out" to bring Daniel understanding (Daniel 9:20–22).

The fact that Gabriel is referred to as a "man" shows that angels are aspects of ourselves. The two phrases "swift flight" and "come out" make this all the more plausible.

The image of Gabriel in swift flight suggests a sudden appearance. Daniel was not consciously evoking the angel, but rather praying to God. The angel Gabriel simply appeared out of nowhere—in other words, Daniel's prayer state opened his ego-centered mind to its angelic faculty. Why? Perhaps, as Daniel says, because he was involved in confessional prayer, an act that deflates and humbles the ego, making it more open to the angelic.

This interpretation is supported by Gabriel's statement that he has now "come out." If Gabriel had descended toward Daniel from the heavens he would have said that he had now "come down." "Coming out" suggests that Gabriel is coming out from Daniel himself, i.e., that he, and all angels, are aspects of human consciousness.

In the Gospel of Luke, Gabriel is again the announcer of the coming transformation. According to Luke, in the days of Herod, the king of Judea, the priest Zechariah was in the Temple in Jerusalem to burn incense:

> Then there appeared to him an angel of the Lord, standing at the right side of the altar of incense. When Zechariah saw him, he was terrified; and fear overwhelmed him. But the angel said to him, "Do not be afraid, Zechariah, for your prayer has been heard. Your

wife Elizabeth will bear you a son, and you will name him John. You will have joy and gladness, and many will rejoice at his birth, for he will be great in the sight of the Lord. He must never drink wine or strong drink; even before his birth he will be filled with the Holy Spirit. He will turn many of the people of Israel to the Lord their God. With the spirit and power of Elijah he will go before him, to turn the hearts of parents to their children, and the disobedient to the wisdom of the righteous, to make ready a people prepared for the Lord." Zechariah said to the angel, "How will I know that this is so? For I am an old man, and my wife is getting on in years." The angel replied, "I am Gabriel. I stand in the presence of God, and I have been sent to speak to you and to bring you this good news. But now, because you did not believe my words, which will be fulfilled in their time, you will become mute, unable to speak, until the day these things occur."

Meanwhile the people were waiting for Zechariah, and wondered at his delay in the sanctuary. When he did come out, he could not speak to them, and they realized that he had seen a vision in the sanctuary. He kept motioning to them and remained unable to speak. When his time of service was ended, he went to his home.

After those days his wife Elizabeth conceived, and for five months she remained in seclusion. She said, "This is what the Lord has done for me when he looked favorably on me and took away the disgrace I have endured among my people."

In the sixth month the angel Gabriel was sent by God to a town in Galilee called Nazareth, to a virgin engaged to a man whose name was Joseph, of the house of David. The virgin's name was Mary. And he came to her and said, "Greetings, favored one! The Lord is with you." But she was much perplexed by his words and pondered what sort of greeting this might be. The angel said to her, "Do not be afraid, Mary, for you have found favor with God. And now, you will conceive in your womb and bear a son, and you will name him Jesus. He will be great, and will be called the Son of the Most High, and the Lord God will give to him the throne of his ancestor David. He will reign over the house of Jacob forever, and of his kingdom there will be no end." Mary said to the angel, "How can this be, since I am a virgin?" The angel said to her, "The Holy Spirit will come upon you, and the power of the Most High will overshadow you; therefore the child to be born will be holy; he will be called Son of God. And now, your relative Elizabeth in her old age has also conceived a son; and this is the sixth month for her who was said to be barren. For nothing will be impossible with God." Then Mary said, "Here am I, the servant of the Lord; let it be with me according to your word." Then the angel departed from her. (Luke 1:11–38)

Gabriel the explainer reveals what God is about to do, while he, himself, does nothing. In the first event a man named John is to be born carrying within him the spirit and power of the prophet Elijah. In the second event a man named Jesus is to be born carrying with him the spirit and power of God. Elijah and Jesus, both of whom are taken bodily into heaven, represent fully God-realized human beings who have attained a higher level of consciousness than the angelic. They have integrated the human and the angelic into a greater whole, the divine.

Gabriel is telling Zechariah and Mary, and through the two of them all of us, that there is a more inclusive unity of human and divine, and that there are individuals among us who have achieved this unity. The fact that Elizabeth is elderly and childless, and Mary is a virgin, were the ways ancient storytellers told their audiences that the children about to be born were unusual, coming from outside the natural way of things, and hence were going to change the world, to bring a new consciousness to bear on humanity.

Of course there are tens of millions of people who read these stories not as myth, as we are doing, but as history. We need not quarrel with this. Our mythic understanding of these events does not deny or affirm their historicity; it only enhances and deepens our understanding of the text when we ask, "What do these texts mean?"

This is the question behind all our investigations into angel myths. We don't ask, "Did this happen?" but "What does it mean?" The meaning of a Virgin Birth or a birth from a barren woman is the same: something deeply transformative is coming into the world, something outside the norm is emerging. And it is this transformation that the angel Gabriel comes to announce.

The angel Jibril plays a comparable role in Islam. He announces not a new birth but a new revelation, and is the voice through which the word of Allah is given to Muhammad. In the Qur'an (53:9) we learn how physically close Jibril was to Muhammad when the Prophet received the Message, and in a Hadith (4:54:455) we are told that Muhammad saw Jibril with six hundred wings.

Ibn Ishaq (d. 767), perhaps the most famous biographer of Muhammad, wrote that Khadijah bint Khuwaylid (d. ca. 618), Muhammad's first wife, sought to test her husband's visions of the angel Jibril to be certain that it was an angel with whom her husband spoke and not a jinn.

She asked Muhammad, "Can you tell me when your Visitor next comes to you?" Muhammad said he could, and Khadijah asked him to do so.

> So when Gabriel came to him, as he was wont, the apostle said to Khadija, 'This is Gabriel who has just come to me.' 'Get up, O son of my uncle,' she said, 'and sit by my left thigh'. The apostle did so, and she said, 'Can you see him?' 'Yes,' he said. She said, 'Then turn round and sit on my right thigh.' He did so, and she said, 'Can you see him?' When he said that he could she asked him to move and sit in her lap. When he had done this she again asked if he could see him, and when he said yes, she disclosed her form and cast aside her veil while the apostle was sitting in her lap. Then she said, 'Can you see him?' And he replied, 'No.' She said, 'O son of my uncle, rejoice and be of good heart, by God he is an angel and not a satan.'[5]

Apparently Jibril fled when Khadijah exposed herself. Given the emphasis on modesty in Abrahamic traditions, we can say that

Jibril fled not from fear of Khadijah, but from fear of being immodest. What Khadijah proved was that Jibril was from God because he placed modesty in high regard. From our perspective what she proved was that Jibril, as a part of Muhammad's unfolding angelic faculty, reflected the Prophet's sense of propriety, reinforcing our contention that angels are not independent of humans but aspects of them.

As in Judaism and Christianity, the Muslim Jibril (or Jibriel) is also primarily a messenger, and, echoing the Gospels, the Qur'an tells us that Jibril informed *Maryam* (Mary) of the conception of *Isa* (Jesus): "She said, 'How can I have a son when no man has touched me? I have not been unchaste,' and he said, 'This is what your Lord said: "It is easy for Me—We shall make him a sign to all people, a blessing from Us"'" (Qur'an 19:20–21).[6]

Muslims also believe that it was Jibril who accompanied Muhammad on his Night Journey (about which we will read in a later chapter).

In summary, Gabriel/Jibril functions most often as an announcer of great transformation, whether it be the Virgin Birth in the New Testament, or the revelation of God to the Prophet Muhammad in and as the Qur'an. An encounter with Gabriel symbolizes that the old ways need mending, and that something new is about to happen in the world.

Raphael

Raphael (Israfil in Islam) is, as his name makes clear, the agent of God's healing—*rofeh* is the Hebrew root for "healing" and "healer." Raphael isn't named in the Jewish biblical canon, though, as we have seen, the rabbis do mention him in the midrash as the angel who accompanied Michael and Gabriel on their visit to Abraham after his circumcision—Raphael was sent to promote Abraham's healing. Midrashic tradition also tells us that Raphael was one of the four angels (along with Michael, Gabriel, and Uriel) sent to lead the Israelite armies, taking his place at the rear of the Israelite formation with the tribe of Ephraim (*Numbers Rabbah* 2:10).

Raphael plays an important role in the *Book of Enoch*, a composite text written over several hundred years, but much of it in the second century BCE. In chapter 22 of this book Enoch tells us that he went to a mountain of solid rock in which there were hollowed out three great caverns with smooth walls. The angel Raphael explains to Enoch that these caverns are the places in which the souls of the dead reside, and in which they await the Day of Final Judgment.

One of the souls of the dead catches Enoch's attention, and Enoch marvels as the soul pleads its case before God. Enoch asks Raphael who this soul is, and learns that it is the soul of Abel, and that he is pleading for the destruction of his brother Cain and all those who descended from him.

Looking at the three caverns, Enoch notices that each is set apart from the others, and inquires of Raphael why this is so. Raphael explains that each of the caverns serves a different function. One is for the righteous who will be rewarded on the Day of Final Judgment, and in it these souls find a spring of clear water. Another is for sinners who die without having tasted justice in life. They will suffer great torment on the Day of Final Judgment. A third is for those who sinned but suffered their punishment while yet alive. They shall stay in this cavern for all eternity but will not suffer on the Day of Final Judgment.

Why is it that Raphael, the angel of healing—rather than, say, Gabriel, the angel most associated with explaining matters to humans—explains Enoch's visions of the underworld? What is the connection between healing and death?

To answer this question we first have to note that the underworld is not Raphael's realm. He is a guide to this world, but not its lord and master. Second, what he reveals to Enoch is the fate of both the good and the wicked, assuring Enoch that there is justice in the grand scheme of things: the good are rewarded and the wicked are punished. Thus Raphael is easing any fear that Enoch may have regarding this issue, and in so doing provides him with a spiritual healing, one that allows Enoch to trust in and bless God all the more fervently. So the healing role for Raphael in the *Book of Enoch* may be more psychological than physical.

Raphael's role as a healer of the flesh is found in the *Book of Tobit* that is part of the Apocrypha.

Tobit lived during the Assyrian exile when Assyria conquered the northern tribes of Israel sometime around 730 BCE. Tobit was a righteous Israelite known for his generosity and honesty, traits that secured him a lucrative position at the court of the Assyrian king in Nineveh.

It was the law in Assyria that the bodies of dead Israelites slain by the king's command were to be left exposed to be eaten by vultures as a sign to others not to challenge the king's rule. Tobit made it his task to secretly bury the bodies of these, his fellow Israelites. When his secret was exposed Tobit was forced to flee for his life, losing all he had.

In time the king was killed, and Tobit's nephew Ahikar became part of the new royal court. Using his influence, Ahikar restored

Tobit to his family and his fortune. His first day back, Tobit sent his son Tobias to invite the neighborhood poor to a feast celebrating his return. As Tobias walked about Nineveh to seek out the poor, he came across the body of a dead Israelite, and ran back to report this to his father. Tobit left his meal untouched and raced out to bring the body to one of his sheds for safekeeping.

At sundown Tobit went out to bury the deceased. Exhausted by the task, he washed himself and lay down by a wall in his courtyard to rest. The night was hot and he lay there with his head unprotected. Sparrows lived in the wall, and their fresh droppings fell into Tobit's eyes, causing a white film to cover them and restrict his vision. Tobit went to doctors for help but their potions made matters worse and he became blind.

Unable to work, Tobit and his family again lost their fortune, living now off the labor of Tobit's wife, Anna. Tobit was so depressed that he prayed for death. Just then he remembered that he had left money in trust in faraway Media. Calling his son to him, Tobit ordered Tobias to go to Media and retrieve the money.

Tobias was not a seasoned traveler and his father sought to hire a guide and bodyguard to protect his son on this journey. The angel Raphael, disguised as an Israelite, presented himself to Tobit and took the job.

On the first night of their journey, Tobias went to wash his feet in the Tigris River. Suddenly a great fish leaped up and swallowed his leg. Crying out for help, Tobias heard Raphael command him to lay hold of the fish and drag it onto dry land. Raphael then instructed Tobias to gut the fish and to save its gall, heart, and liver as medicine.

Tobias inquired as to the medicinal powers of the fish, and the angel Raphael, still in disguise, explained that when burned the heart and liver would give off a smoke that could free the possessed from the demons that haunt them, and that when placed on the eyes the gall could heal the blind whose blindness was caused by bird droppings.

When Tobias and Raphael arrive in Media, Raphael convinces Tobias to stay at the home of Raguel, a relative of Tobias (and no relation to the angel Raguel mentioned in *Enoch*). Raguel has a beautiful daughter named Sarah who is still single, and Raphael suggests that Tobias marry her.

But Tobias objects. He has heard that this Sarah is a serial killer. Seven times was she married, and seven times her husbands fell dead before consummating the marriage. What no one knows, no one except the angel Raphael, is that Sarah is being stalked by the Demon King Asmodeus, who desires Sarah for himself and has been killing off the competitors.

Raphael urges Tobias to ask for Sarah's hand in marriage, and, despite his fears, Tobias does. Sarah's father consents to the union. Raphael then instructs Tobias to burn the heart and liver of the great fish he had caught (or rather, which had caught him) in the censor of his bedroom before Sarah comes there to join him. The stench is so offensive to the Demon King that as soon as he enters the room to murder Tobias he is forced to run from the bedchamber and keeps running until he has reached the far end of Egypt. There Raphael attacks him, and binds him hand and foot.

Tobias returns with Sarah to Nineveh, places the fish gall onto Tobit's eyes, and thus restores his father's vision.

At the end of the story (*Tobit* 12:14–15) Raphael reveals his true identity to Tobit and his son. "I am Raphael, one of the seven angels attending before the glory of God, ever ready to do His bidding. I was commissioned to appraise you, and to heal Sarah, your son's wife."

When Raphael reveals himself the two men fall on their faces seemingly in worship. The Jewish author of the *Book of Tobit*, for whom the worship of angels is anathema, makes it clear that such worship is not appropriate. Raphael says to them (*Tobit* 12:20–22), "Stand up and acknowledge God! Behold! I am returning to the One who sent me. Record all these events you have witnessed." Tobit and his son stand up, but Raphael has already risen so high that he can no longer be seen. The two men begin to bless God, and sing hymns to him, and they bear witness and give thanks to God for the wonders that had befallen them when the angel Raphael had come to them.

Raphael in the *Book of Tobit* is the angel of healing, yet he acts in a hidden manner disguised as a human and working through the agency of human beings, suggesting once more that angels are not beings in and of themselves, but levels of consciousness that we humans can obtain.

Uriel

Uriel means "Light of God," and this archangel was understood to be one of the ways God's wisdom could be made known to us. In Judaism he is associated with the *TaNaKH*, the acronym for the three sections of the Hebrew Bible: Torah, Nevi'im, and Ketuvim (the Five Books of Moses, the Prophets, and the Writings). Why was he named Uriel? Because of the Torah, the Prophets, and the Writings by means of which the Holy One, blessed be He, atones for sins and gives light (*ur*) to Israel (*Numbers Rabbah* 2:10).

While Uriel is not mentioned in the New Testament, and also

does not appear in Islam, he had a certain presence. And despite his demotion from archangel to saint by Pope Zachary in 745, Uriel must have maintained a following among the people. In the tenth century, for example, a Bulgarian heresy called Bogomilism arose in opposition to what it felt was an oppressive church hierarchy. Bogomilism returned Uriel to his status as archangel, and it may have been the growing popularity of the Bogomils that caused Pope Clement III in the late twelfth century to order all images of Uriel removed from the churches.

Uriel, who is also called *Phanuel*, "Face of God," since God is imagined as pure and blinding light, plays a major role in the *Fourth Book of Ezra* (also referred to as *2 Esdras*). This apocryphal text is part of the *Pseudepigrapha*, a word derived from the Greek *pseudes* (false) and *epigraphe* (inscription). Pseudepigrapha are texts that falsely claim to be authored by famous figures from the past. Claiming such authorship was not an act of trickery, but of modesty. The actual authors felt they were speaking the wisdom of the ancients and should give credit where credit is due.

In the case of the *Fourth Book of Ezra* the credit is given to Ezra, the fifth-century BCE Israelite priest and scribe whose religious reforms set the stage for the revival of Judaism that would emerge after the end of the Babylonian exile around 538 BCE.

The book itself, composed around the year 100 CE, was written to address the concerns of the Jews whose Temple had been utterly destroyed by the Romans some thirty years earlier. Rather than address the issue head on, however, the author revives the character of Ezra who was instrumental in rebuilding the Temple after its first destruction in 586 BCE. Together Ezra and the archangel Uriel explore the meaning of the First Temple's destruction and thus, by extension, that of the Second Temple as well. Uriel says, "I have been sent to show you three puzzles. If you can solve one of them for me, I will then show you what you desire to see, and will teach you why the heart is evil . . . Go and weigh for me the weight of fire, or measure for me a blast of wind, or call back for me the day that is past . . ."[7]

Uriel makes clear the need for angelic intervention: without Uriel, the Light of God, the ego-centered mind is in the dark. Yet Uriel doesn't simply shine the light of truth on us, he challenges us to solve puzzles, to earn our way to the light by exercising our imagination.

This is very important. The light of God is available to us only when we have learned to use our mental faculties creatively. God—"I will be whatever I will be"—is pure creativity, and we, made in the image and likeness of God, must ourselves become creative. Solving Uriel's puzzles is the way this challenge plays out in the *Fourth Book of Ezra*.

Ezra replies to Uriel by saying,

> "Be not angry with those who are deemed worse than beasts; but love those who have always put their trust in your glory. For we and our fathers have passed our lives in ways that bring death, but you, because of us sinners, are called merciful . . . For the righteous who have many works laid up with you shall receive their reward in consequence of their own deeds. But what is man that you are angry with him or what is a mortal race that you are so bitter against it? For in truth there is no one among those who have been born who hasn't acted wickedly . . . There is no one who has not transgressed. For in this, O Lord, your righteousness and

goodness will be declared when you are merciful to those who have no good works."[8]

It is clear from this passage that Ezra is addressing God through the archangel Uriel, and thus is providing us with a strong example in support of our premise that angels are faculties of the human mind that allow us to transcend the ego-centered mind toward God-centered spirit.

It is also worth noting that Ezra's questioning of Uriel mirrors the psalmist's question to God, "What is humanity, that You remember them? And the children of humanity, that You are mindful of them?" (Psalm 8:4). Ezra says, "But what is man that you are angry with him or what is a mortal race that you are so bitter against it?" The Psalmist sees a God who is concerned with humanity and eager to see us succeed. Ezra envisions an angry God who is bitterly disappointed in humanity.

These two texts, separated by centuries, reflect two different political realities. The Psalmist was writing at the time of Israel's independence under King David, while the author of Ezra was writing as Jerusalem fell to Rome and the next great exile began. It is an act of audacious hope on the part of the author of the *Fourth Book of Ezra* to use the historical Ezra as his foil. The real Ezra lived as the Babylonian exile was coming to an end and the Jewish people were reconstructing their homeland. To put these painful words into Ezra's mouth when in fact the historical Ezra would be far more optimistic about Israel's future is yet another twist of this book.

Ezra is making the case that God's obsession with those few humans who are truly wicked is misplaced. God should recall those who did right in his eyes. Similarly, if God wishes to be known for mercy, why focus on the mistakes all people make? Forgive instead. Yet Uriel, and by extension God, is unmoved, telling Ezra, "For this is the way of which Moses, while he was alive, spoke to the people, saying 'Choose for yourselves life, that you may live!' But they did not believe him, or the prophets after him . . . Therefore there shall not be grief at their damnation, or much joy over those to whom salvation is assured."[9]

God's justice trumps his mercy in the *Fourth Book of Ezra*. Why? Because the Second Temple has been destroyed, a fact that the author cannot mention but also cannot ignore. Yet the author cannot leave us bereft. While each of the four archangels has his own role to play, at the end of time, on Judgment Day, Michael, Gabriel, Raphael, and Uriel will gather again to bring the wicked to justice, those who served Satan in order to mislead humankind.

While the judgment of the agents of Satan is assured, Satan himself seems to escape unscathed. Is this optimistic or pessimistic? Wouldn't it be better if Satan were defeated?

Better, perhaps, but not realistic. Satan is the shadow side of narrow ego-centered mind. If Ezra can stand before Uriel, the Light of God, behind him will of necessity be Satan, the Shadow of God. Light and Dark cannot be separated—a truth that the ego-centered mind cannot grasp, and which the angelic potential of humans cannot deny.

Five

Satan, the Fallen Angel

IF ANGELS ARE a mythopoetic way of addressing the human potential to open to greater and more inclusive levels of consciousness,
what are we to make of Satan? In essence, Satan, as a quasi-
independent angelic force, represents the misdirection of the ego-
centered mind to use its angelic potential not to transcend itself, but
to reinforce itself and the painful and angst-ridden state of *achad* by
which it defines itself.

Such misdirected angelic potential can be traced back, according
to Harold Bloom in *Fallen Angels*, to the sacred writings of Zoroastrianism, the religion of Babylonia that introduced the Jews, and

through them Christians and Muslims, to the idea of personified evil: "Satan proper, who became crucial to Christianity, was not a Jewish but a Persian idea, invented by Zoroaster (Zarathustra) more than a thousand years before the time of the historical Jesus."[1]

Ahriman

Ahriman, who is also called *Arimanius* and *Angra Mainyu*, is the evil opponent of *Ahura Mazda*, the Lord of Light, in the ancient religion of Zoroastrianism. It is he who leads the evil angels in a cosmic war against the good angels.

According to Zoroastrian mythology, Ahura Mazda told Zoroaster that his intension was to make a paradise on earth where humans would, by their own free will, choose to do what is right and good. But Ahriman took delight in getting people to choose just the opposite.

Ahriman introduced extreme selfishness into the human psyche as a means of manipulating humans to make wrong choices. In other words, he is the source of the misdirection of the ego-centered mind, having its innate desire for self-transcendence perverted in a desire for self-inflation. Here we understand him not as a physical entity, but as the evil potential within us.

According to the Gathas, the sacred hymns of Zoroaster, Ahriman/Angra Mainyu, the Hostile Spirit, was in the beginning clearly distinct from Spenta Mainyu, the Good Spirit governing humanity. Angra Mainyu, however, sought to bridge the gap between them and enter the realm of the Good. At first his efforts failed, and Ahura Mazda kept him at bay. But in time the Lord of Light realized that this battle with Angra Mainyu would go on forever, and therefore decided to allow Angra Mainyu a place in the realm of the Good, and in this way to trap him once and for all. This is how the selfish, evil spirit came to play a role in the human psyche, and while we must be vigilant against the misdirection of Ahriman/Angra Mainyu, we can be certain that in the end Ahurah Mazda will prevail.

The *Book of Arda Viraf*, written sometime between the third and seventh centuries BCE, describes the dream-journey of Viraf, a devout follower of the prophet Zoroaster, to heaven. In heaven Viraf meets Ahurah Mazda and learns of "the reality of God and the archangels, and the nonreality of Ahriman and the demons" (5:10).[2] This means that following the advice of Ahriman and moving more deeply into I-It consciousness further alienates the individual from the nondual reality that is the ground of all being.

Satan in the Hebrew Bible and in Rabbinic Midrash

The Hebrew root *stn* from which the word Satan derives means "one who opposes, obstructs, or acts as adversary." This is equivalent to the Greek word *diabolos* from which we derive the English "devil." A *diabolos* is "one who tosses something across one's path to block it." Satan makes only a few appearances in the Hebrew Bible, and, unlike Ahriman in Zoroastrian mythology, nowhere appears as an autonomous enemy of God, but rather acts at God's behest, or, at worst, as an agent provocateur. What follows is an example of the latter.

In the first book of Chronicles, "Satan opposed Israel and urged David to take a census of the people Israel" (1 Chronicles 21:1). The taking of this census angered God, and David was presented with a terrible dilemma:

> YHVH addressed David's prophet, Gad, and said: "Go
> to David and say to him, 'YHVH says choose: three

years of famine, three months of destruction by your enemies' swords, or three days of YHVH's sword—a plague upon the land and YHVH's angel wreaking havoc throughout Israel.' Decide now that I might report back to the one who sent me." David replied to Gad, "I am shattered, but let me fall into YHVH's hands rather than those of humans." So YHVH unleashed a plague upon Israel that took the lives of seventy thousand. (1 Chronicles 21:9–14)

The death of seventy thousand Israelites is a horror, and not the only one that we find in the Bible. And the fact that the Bible presents it as a sign of God's mercy is also troubling. On the other hand the Bible makes it clear that David, and not Satan, is responsible for the census and the horror that results from it. David himself, while pleading for God to end the massacre, says, "I alone ordered the census of the people. I alone have sinned and sinned badly. But these sheep, where is their guilt? YHVH, my God! Let your hand crush me and my father's house, but spare your people this plague!" (1 Chronicles 21:17).

Clearly at this point in the imagination of Israel Satan cannot make people do things; he can only suggest them. We see something similar in Zechariah's vision of Joshua opposed by Satan: "Then he showed me Joshua, the High Priest, standing before the angel of God, and Satan was standing on his right to accuse him. The angel of God said to Satan, 'May God denounce you, O Satan! May God, who chooses Jerusalem, denounce you!'" (Zechariah 3:1–2).

Joshua the high priest was part of the exiled Jewish leadership taken into Babylonian captivity in 586 BCE. Zechariah's vision tells of a time when the exiled leaders will return to Jerusalem and reestablish worship and sacrifice in the Temple. When the exiles were allowed to return they were not welcomed with open arms. The Jews who had remained behind were not eager to see the old guard returned to power. Zechariah, writing during this difficult time in Israel's history, had Satan stand in for those Jews who resisted the return to power of the former exiles.

Two things are important to note here. First, we are once again shown that the power of Satan is limited to suggestions and murmurings: Satan opposes Joshua but does not and cannot stop him. Second, we are witnessing a new phenomenon in Jewish life: the association of one's enemies with Satan. Never before had one group of Jews linked an opposing group of Jews with Satan. This change was to have grave consequences, beginning with the Gospels and continuing throughout Christendom.

In the book of Job, Satan has taken on the role of God's "prosecutor":

> One day the divine beings assembled before God and Satan came with them. God asked Satan, "Where have you been?" Satan replied, "I have been roaming the earth." God said, "Did you notice my servant Job? There is no one like him on earth, blameless and upright, fearing God and shunning evil."
>
> Satan replied to God, "Doesn't Job have good reason to fear God? You have shielded him all about. Him, and his family, and his possession. You have blessed his every endeavor and his holdings spread out over the land. Lay waste to any of these and he will curse You to Your Face!"

"Let us see if this is so," said God. "All that he has is now under your control, only do not harm Job himself." Satan departed from the presence of God. (Job 1:6–12)

It is important to note that it is God here, not Satan, who introduces Job into the conversation. Satan simply tells God that he had been scouring the earth doing his job. God, however, is not interested in Satan's findings; instead God wants to make sure that Satan did take notice of Job who loves God more than any other on earth.

It is clear to Satan that God is fishing for a compliment. Being the leader of the loyal opposition, Satan can't resist poking fun at God's need for this human admirer. Job loves God, so Satan argues, because God loves Job. Change God's side of the equation and Job's side will change as well.

God's need for validation rather than Satan's lust for inflicting pain is the motivation behind the myth. Satan does as God commands, destroying Job's property and killing his children, but Job still clings to his love of God. God, feeling validated, throws this in Satan's face. Rising to the challenge, Satan says that Job's love of God is still contingent on the fact that Satan was not allowed to cause Job himself physical pain. Again God is goaded to test Job, and Satan torments Job physically, afflicting him with "severe boils from the soles of his feet to the top of his head" (Job 2:7).

Seeing her husband sitting among the ashes of his former wealth, and scratching his sores with a broken piece of clay pottery, Job's wife says, "Do you still cling to your righteousness? Curse God and die!" (Job 2:9). Job looks at her and says, "You speak as one of the impious women. Should we accept the good from God and not accept the evil as well?" (Job 2:10).

At this point the book of Job shifts from a myth about Satan to one of the most profound and poetic explorations of the nature of God's justice anywhere in human literature. Satan's role is finished, and Job, his friends, and God play out the rest of the story, until at the end Job receives back his health, wealth, and family.

One last example from the Hebrew Bible will suffice to make clear that here Satan is not an autonomous agent of evil, but rather a loyal servant of God. Recalling that the Hebrew *stn* and the Greek *diabolos* refer to one who obstructs, the myth of Balaam's donkey in the book of Numbers shows how the obstructive nature of Satan, as one of God's angels, can be in the service of the good.

Balaam is a prophet who has been charged by his king, Balak of Moab, to curse the people Israel and in this way strengthen the king's hand in the coming battle with the Israelites. Although not himself an Israelite, Balaam is a servant of YHVH, and it is to YHVH that he turns for guidance. At first God tells Balaam not to follow the king's order, but then God changes his mind, and commands Balaam to do as he was told by King Balak, but to speak only such words as God himself instructs him to speak:

> When Balaam awoke in the morning, he saddled his donkey, and accompanied the Moabite officials. God was furious at Balaam's going, so an angel of YHVH stood in the road to oppose him. He [Balaam] was riding on his donkey flanked by two servants. When the donkey saw the angel of YHVH standing in the road, his sword in his hand, she turned aside from the road

into a field. Balaam struck the donkey to bring her back to the road. Then the angel of YHVH positioned himself on a narrow path between the vineyards flanked by walls on both sides. Seeing the angel of YHVH, the donkey pressed against the wall scraping Balaam's foot alongside it. So he beat her again. Then the angel of YHVH moved closer and stood in a place so narrow there was no room to swerve either to the right or to the left. When the donkey saw the angel of YHVH, she lay down under Balaam, kindling his anger so that he beat her with his staff. At that moment YHVH opened the donkey's mouth and she spoke to Balaam, "What did I do to deserve these three beatings?" Balaam said to the donkey, "You mock me! If I had a sword with me I'd kill you!" The donkey replied, "Aren't I the same donkey you have ridden all your life? Is it my habit to treat you this way?" Balaam replied, "No."

Just then YHVH opened Balaam's eyes, and he saw the angel of YHVH standing, sword drawn, in the road. He dropped to the ground and prostrated himself. The angel of YHVH said to him, "Three times you have beaten your donkey, why? I have come out as an adversary, because your action is abhorrent to me. The donkey saw me, and sought to avoid me three times. Had she not done so, I would have killed you and let her live." Then Balaam said to the angel of YHVH, "I was mistaken, and did not know you were standing here opposing me. If you still oppose me, I will go back." The angel of YHVH said to Balaam, "Go with these men, but say only what I tell you to say." So Balaam continued on with Balak's officers. (Numbers 22:21–35)

While it is puzzling that God would tell Balaam to do as Balak commands, but then sends his angel to block Balaam's path, it is clear that the angel is acting as *diabolos*, the way blocker, and is doing so clearly at the behest of God. As Elaine Pagels writes in *The Origin of Satan*,

> In the Hebrew Bible, as in mainstream Judaism to this day, Satan never appears as Western Christendom has come to know him, as the leader of an "evil empire," an army of hostile spirits who make war on God and humankind alike. As he first appears in the Hebrew Bible, Satan is not necessarily evil, much less opposed to God. On the contrary, he appears in the book of Numbers and in Job as one of God's obedient servants—a messenger, or *angel* . . .
>
> In biblical sources the Hebrew term the *satan* describes an adversarial role. It is not the name of a particular character. Although Hebrew storytellers as early as the sixth century B.C.E. occasionally introduced a supernatural character whom they called the *satan*, what they meant was any one of the angels sent by God for the specific purpose of blocking or obstructing human activity.
>
> The *satan*'s presence in a story could help account for unexpected obstacles or reversals of fortune . . .

Some, however, also invoke this supernatural character, the *satan*, who, by God's own order or permission, blocks or opposes human plans and desires. But this messenger is not necessarily malevolent. God sends him, like the angel of death, to perform a specific task, although one that human beings may not appreciate . . . Thus the *satan* may simply have been sent by the Lord to protect a person from worse harm.[3]

In other words, the biblical—and rabbinic—authors use the idea of Satan to add drama to their stories and make sudden plot twists and shifts, and never imagined a malevolent force similar to Ahriman/Angra Mainyu in Zoroastrianism or the Devil as he developed in Christianity. Seeing Satan as a literary device, however, doesn't mean that he has no relevance to our understanding of angels as symbols of the human capacity to move back and forth between levels of consciousness. In this context the Jewish Satan represents blocks that we may face when attempting such a move. As in the story of Balaam's donkey, these blocks need not always be overcome but are sent by God to ensure we act in accord with justice and compassion. Satan as the Adversary allows us the opportunity to stop and confront the motives behind our actions, encourages us to use the insights we glean from higher levels of consciousness to expand the presence of justice and compassion in the lower realms.

• • •

According to rabbinic midrash, on the day Isaac was born Abraham held a great feast, inviting all the chieftains and their wives to join him in celebrating the birth of Sarah's son. It was the custom in those days to invite the poor to such a feast, but in his enthusiasm over Isaac's birth Abraham forgot to do so. It was a rabbinic teaching that when there are no poor at a banquet Satan comes in their stead. And so Satan came to Abraham's tent dressed as a poor man seeking bread.

As we have seen, in the Hebrew Bible Satan is not a fallen angel but a loyal if skeptical servant of the Divine Judge. Satan's task is to roam the earth (Job 1:7) to observe the doings of humans and report his findings to God. Satan cannot make people do evil; his task is simply to let God know the evil that people choose to do.

Because Abraham had forgotten to invite the poor to his celebration, Satan attended the banquet as a beggar to see if Abraham and Sarah would be hospitable to the poor had they remembered to invite them in the first place. But Abraham was so occupied with his important guests that he never saw the "beggar" and bade him no welcome. Sarah, too, never noticed the beggar for she was deep in argument with the other wives and mothers present trying to convince them that Isaac was indeed her son and not that of another concubine.

Satan waited a while but departed empty-handed. At the next gathering of God and his angels he reported what he had seen. Satan charged Abraham with the sin of inhospitality and demanded that his faith be tested. God agreed and staged the near sacrifice of Isaac.[4]

The divine call for Isaac's death mirrors the divine saving of Ishmael's life (when his mother Hagar had been forced to take him into the desert), and speaks to the unpredictable nature of God: "I will be what I will be; sometimes life giving, sometimes life taking." Yet God's creativity, at least in the minds of the rabbis, is not random or haphazard. There has to be an opening through which God's creativity can act. The Bible is silent regarding what kind of opening would allow God to command Abraham to kill Isaac, but the rabbis are quick to fill in the gaps.

First, as we have seen, there is the matter of Abraham and Sarah's ignoring the "beggar." But while this might warrant some punishment of Abraham and Sarah, it does not provide an opening for the sacrifice of Isaac. So another story is woven in.

According to this midrash, Ishmael once boasted of his courage to his little brother Isaac saying, "When I was thirteen our father cut off my foreskin in accordance with the will of God and I did not hesitate or protest." Not to be outdone Isaac replied, "What is a bit of skin and the pain of its removal? My courage is greater than yours for if God commanded our father to take not a bit of skin but my entire life I would offer it without hesitation."[5] Here was the opening God needed to test Abraham through his son Isaac.

Satan, wanting to make sure that Abraham and Sarah suffered, but having no interest in the death of Isaac, did what he could to prevent Abraham from completing his task. As Abraham and Isaac walked toward Mount Moriah where the sacrifice was to take place, Satan appeared to Abraham in the form of an old and humble sage.

"Are you so foolish as to believe God wishes you to kill the son through whom your legacy lies? This thing does not come from God. Go home and be done with it." But Abraham recognized the old man as Satan and rebuked him, and Satan departed.

Failing to fool Abraham in his old-man disguise, Satan appeared to Isaac as a young man to convince him to reject his father's plan and return home to his mother. Isaac took counsel with his father, and Abraham again recognized Satan and rebuked him.

Seeing that he could not stop Abraham with logic, Satan sought to block his way with magic. He transformed himself into a raging river and cut off the road to Moriah. Abraham, Isaac, and the two servants who accompanied them sought to cross the river but sank up to their necks and were about to drown. Abraham then realized that this too was the work of Satan, and he said, "I have passed this way many times and never was there a river here before. This is the work of Satan." Thus Satan fled, leaving a passable road behind him.

Satan then appeared to Sarah and sought to enlist her help in stopping Abraham from killing her only child. The thought of her murdered son sent her into shock and she died, but with her dying breath she said to Satan, "All that God has told Abraham, may he do it for life and peace!"[6] With this Satan abandoned his attempts to stop Abraham from carrying out the will of God.

Sarah's words are crucial to understanding the deeper meaning of this story. Satan here represents that aspect of ourselves that resists change. Isaac symbolizes hope and the future. Abraham is called to kill that future, that is to say God is challenging Abraham to realize that no one can predict the creative unfolding of the divine process. Abraham thought he knew his destiny and that of his son Isaac, but here he is seeking to take the very life of the one who was to carry life forward. It makes no sense, and cannot make sense because Abraham cannot know the future, only the past and the present. What Abraham is really called to sacrifice is the illusion of surety and security that comes from the delusion that he is somehow in control of his destiny.

What is asked of Abraham is asked of each of us. We have to act in the present without knowing what comes next. How do we determine how to act? Sarah tells us with her dying breath: act for life and for peace. Abraham has to trust that God will only act for life and for peace, though doing so, as we have seen, often entails death and destruction.

Satan in the Pseudepigrapha and in the Gospels

The evil understanding of Satan comes into Jewish life through the Pseudepigrapha, written between 200 BCE and 200 CE (see page 107).

Satan as the chief of the fallen angels makes his first appearance in the *Second or Slavonic Book of Enoch*, written perhaps in the first century BCE or first century CE. In this text we find the following brief myth: "Satan was hurled from the heights, together with his angels. But one from the order of the archangels deviated, together with the division that was under his authority. He thought up the impossible idea that he might place his throne higher than the clouds which are above the earth, and that he might become equal to My power. And I [God] hurled him out from the height, together with his angels. And he was flying around in the air, ceaselessly, above the Bottomless."[7]

In the *Martyrdom and Ascension of Isaiah*, a book of pseudepigrapha written perhaps in the first century CE, we find Satan conspiring to bring down King Manasseh.

The book deals in part with the reign of the seventh-century BCE King Manasseh, considered one of the worst of the Israelite kings. The Bible tells us that Manasseh "did what was evil in the eyes of God" (2 Kings 21:2)—he erected altars to Baal, practiced astrology, read omens, performed necromancy, conjured up spirits, and shed so much innocent blood that Jerusalem flowed with it "from end to end" (2 Kings 21:16). But the Bible itself does not assign or associate

Manasseh's evil with Satan. For that we need to look to the *Martyr-dom and Ascension of Isaiah*, which, like other texts from the period, refers to Satan by the name Samael (part of a general confusion of the two angels in both Jewish and Christian literature, arising from the fact that Samael often plays the role of the accuser, *satan* in Hebrew; nevertheless Samael is distinct from Satan, and is often understood as the angel of death): "And Samael [Satan] dwelt in Manasseh and clung closely to him. And Manasseh abandoned the service of the Lord of his father and served Satan, and his angels and his powers."[8]

Important here is the association of Manasseh with the Devil, since Manasseh is not an outsider, nor an enemy of Israel or Israel's God. Manasseh is a king, and yet he turns to the Devil rather than God. This notion that Satan conspires with elements of one's own people to destroy that people's relationship with God allows civil strife to take on the elements of a cosmic struggle. As Elaine Pagels says, "Satan is not the distant enemy but the intimate enemy—one's trusted colleague, close associate, brother. He is the kind of person on whose loyalty and goodwill the well-being of family and society depend—but one who turns unexpectedly jealous and hostile."[9]

. . .

Satan as "intimate enemy" is found in Jesus's rebuke of Peter in the Gospel of Matthew. "Jesus began to show his disciples that he must go to Jerusalem and undergo great suffering at the hands of the elders and chief priests and scribes, and be killed, and on the third day be raised" (Matthew 16:21). Peter is appalled at the thought of this and rebukes Jesus. Jesus then turns to Peter and says, "Get behind me, Satan! You are a stumbling block to me; for you are setting your mind not on divine things but on human things" (Matthew 16:23).

Here Peter is still playing the role of the *diabolos*, the obstructer. He is not Satan per se, but articulating the satanic, the obstructive fear that arises within him at the thought of Jesus's passion and death. But to call Peter Satan is new, and quite alien to the Hebrew Bible.

Something similar is revealed in the Gospel of Luke where we read about Judas's betrayal of Jesus: "Then Satan entered into Judas called Iscariot, who was one of the twelve; he went away and conferred with the chief priests and officers of the temple police about how he might betray him to them" (Luke 22:3–4).

At first this may sound like the Satan in the Chronicles story of David and the census, but looking closer it becomes clear that Satan possesses Judas in some way, and, rather than approaching Judas with the suggestion that he betray his teacher, actually takes over the body of Judas to do the betraying. Indeed, this passage in Luke may be the first time in biblical literature that the notion appears that Satan can enter into a person and use that person for satanic ends.

Satan again enters into Judas in the Gospel of John where, after partaking of the Last Supper, Judas becomes possessed and Jesus says to him, or more accurately to the Satan within him, "Do quickly what you are going to do" (John 13:27).

Earlier in John's Gospel Jesus seems to equate those Jews who oppose him with the Devil: "If God were your Father, you would love me, for I came from God . . . You are from your father the devil, and you choose to do your father's desires" (John 8:42–44).

Linking the Jews to the Devil has had grave consequences for both Jews and Christians over many centuries, but even a cursory exploration of this would take us too far afield. Nor is this politicized Devil the primary myth of Satan in the New Testament. Far beyond the polemic against those Jews who opposed Jesus, the Gospels present us with an otherworldly Satan echoing the evil Ahriman of Zoroastrianism, far removed from the loyal opponent in Jewish literature.

In the Gospel of John, for example, we learn that Satan is the "ruler of this world" (John 12:31), and in Matthew's Gospel Satan tempts Jesus in hopes of derailing his mission:

> Then Jesus was led up by the Spirit into the wilderness to be tempted by the devil. He fasted forty days and forty nights, and afterwards he was famished. The tempter came and said to him, "If you are the Son of God, command these stones to become loaves of bread." But he answered, "It is written, 'One does not live by bread alone, but by every word that comes from the mouth of God.'"
>
> Then the devil took him to the holy city and placed him on the pinnacle of the temple, saying to him, "If you are the Son of God, throw yourself down; for it is written, 'He will command his angels concerning you,' and 'On their hands they will bear you up, so that you will not dash your foot against a stone.'" Jesus said to him, "Again it is written, 'Do not put the Lord your God to the test.'"
>
> Again, the devil took him to a very high mountain and showed him all the kingdoms of the world and their splendor; and he said to him, "All these I will give you, if you will fall down and worship me." Jesus said to him, "Away with you, Satan! for it is written,

'Worship the Lord your God, and serve only him.'"
Then the devil left him, and suddenly angels came and
waited on him. (Matthew 4:1–11)

Another account of this story is found in the Gospel according to
Luke:

Jesus, full of the Holy Spirit, returned from the Jordan
and was led by the Spirit in the wilderness, where for
forty days he was tempted by the devil. He ate nothing
at all during those days, and when they were over, he
was famished. The devil said to him, "If you are the
Son of God, command this stone to become a loaf of
bread." Jesus answered him, "It is written, 'One does
not live by bread alone.'"

Then the devil led him up and showed him in an
instant all the kingdoms of the world. And the devil
said to him, "To you I will give their glory and all this
authority; for it has been given over to me, and I give it
to anyone I please. If you, then, will worship me, it will
all be yours." Jesus answered him, "It is written, 'Worship the Lord your God, and serve only him.'"

Then the devil took him to Jerusalem, and placed
him on the pinnacle of the temple, saying to him, "If
you are the Son of God, throw yourself down from
here, for it is written, 'He will command his angels
concerning you, to protect you,' and 'On their hands
they will bear you up, so that you will not dash your
foot against a stone.'" Jesus answered him, "It is said,
'Do not put the Lord your God to the test.'" When the

devil had finished every test, he departed from him until an opportune time. (Luke 4:1–13)

Satan is not acting in accordance with God's will, nor does he need any human agent to carry out his will. Yet Satan in the Gospels is still not like the mighty cosmic Ahriman/Angra Mainyu in Zoroastrianism. There is no cosmic war in the Gospels between Jesus as the Lord of Light and an Ahriman-like Lord of Darkness. Satan in these temptation stories is still much more of an inner demon, an "intimate enemy." As Christianity develops, however, Satan does indeed become much more so the powerful cosmic enemy of God.

• • •

Like Jesus in the desert, the Buddha, too, is tempted by a devil-like character, *Mara*.

Mara is essentially a tempter who seeks to distract humans from their spiritual practices, and entices them with mundane affairs. Early Buddhists saw Mara as a nuisance who, while existing in his own realm, manifested within the human mind as the inner voice of temptation. The Pali Canon, the oldest canonical texts of Buddhism, provide several encounters between the Buddha and Mara, the most important dealing with the Buddha's enlightenment.

Having decided to forsake his princely life and pursue enlightenment, Siddhartha Gotama, the historical Buddha, left home and took up with a band of *sadhus*, forest-dwelling ascetics with whom he lived and practiced austerities for six years. Mara, fearing that Siddhartha was progressing spiritually, sought to dissuade him from his practice. Mara said to Siddhartha,

You are so thin and pale,
That you are close to death.
A thousand parts are pledged to death,
And only one part still holds to life.
Live, Sir! Life is better than death.
In life you can gain merit [toward a better rebirth].
Come, live the Holy Life and pour out libations on
    the holy fires,
And thus earn much merit.
What can you gain from your struggles?
This path of struggle is too rough, and difficult, and
    hard to bear.[10]

Siddhartha recognized the temptations of Mara for what they were, distractions from his true path. He rebuked Mara and maintained his practice, reminding the tempter, and perhaps himself, that "I have faith (*saddha*), strength (*viriya*) and wisdom (*panna*)."[11] And Mara himself acknowledged that "for seven years I pursued the Buddha at every step, yet with the wakeful Buddha I got no chance . . . In disgust I give up my efforts to thwart this Gotama."[12]

Following his enlightenment the Buddha spent seven weeks in meditation and fasting during which time the Daughters of Mara tried to talk him out of teaching others how to achieve enlightenment. But they, too, failed.

The Buddha does not slay Mara or his daughters. He, like Jesus in his temptation, is simply not persuaded by them. In both stories the Tempter actually helps us clarify what is important. The Buddha and Jesus recognize the darkness for what it is and neither fear it nor project it onto others. They are simply not moved by it. While other sages clearly see Satan as the physical enemy to be destroyed, Jesus and Buddha see Satan/Mara as an inner temptation to be rejected.

This is central to how we are to deal with our own dark side. We have to listen to what it has to say, and then choose *not* to do what it wants us to do.

Yet it is important to notice that both the Buddha and Jesus *are* tempted. In other words, they are not beyond the reach of Mara or Satan, but they are not entrapped by them. Why? Because the Buddha and Jesus acknowledge that Mara and Satan are an undeniable part of themselves. Both Jesus and the Buddha represent the fully human being who realizes that everything is part of the One who is God.

Satan in Revelation, Later Christian Texts, and in Islam

As we have seen, Satan in the Hebrew Bible is a loyal servant of God, but over the centuries he evolves into God's enemy. John of Patmos, in the book of Revelation, describes a new Satan almost equal in power to God. This development continues in later Christian writings, where Satan/the Devil is associated with those who oppose Christianity.

The book of Revelation is an important example of apocalyptic, symbol-filled literature, where Satan appears as the dragon waiting to devour the child about to be birthed by the woman clothed in the sun. The dragon fails in his effort, as the child and his mother are rescued by God. Then war breaks out in heaven (see page 86), with the archangel Michael leading those loyal to God against the rebel angels led by Satan (Revelation 12:7–9). But Satan cannot conquer heaven, so he now seeks to conquer earth, at least until the return of Christ. The following verses describe Satan's beast and his evil army and their final assault against the armies of heaven on horseback:

> Then I saw heaven opened, and there was a white horse! Its rider is called Faithful and True, and in righteousness he judges and makes war. His eyes are like a flame of fire, and on his head are many diadems; and he has a name inscribed that no one knows but himself. He is clothed in a robe dipped in blood, and his name is called The Word of God. And the armies of heaven, wearing fine linen, white and pure, were following him on white horses. From his mouth comes a sharp sword with which to strike down the nations, and he will rule them with a rod of iron; he will tread the wine press of the fury of the wrath of God the Almighty. On his robe and on his thigh he has a name inscribed, "King of kings and Lord of lords."
>
> Then I saw an angel standing in the sun, and with a loud voice he called to all the birds that fly in mid-heaven, "Come, gather for the great supper of God, to eat the flesh of kings, the flesh of captains, the flesh of the mighty, the flesh of horses and their riders—flesh of all, both free and slave, both small and great." Then I saw the beast and the kings of the earth with their armies gathered to make war against the rider on the horse and against his army. And the beast was captured, and with it the false prophet who had performed in its presence the signs by which he deceived those who had received the mark of the beast and those who worshiped its image. These two were thrown alive into

the lake of fire that burns with sulfur. And the rest
were killed by the sword of the rider on the horse, the
sword that came from his mouth; and all the birds were
gorged with their flesh. (Revelation 19:11–21)

The book of Revelation shows clearly the Zoroastrian-inspired
dualism that captured the imagination of the early Christian writers.
But what are we to make of the myth in Revelation? If Satan is the
misdirected energy of ego-centered mind, used not to transcend itself
but to entrench itself all the more deeply in the dualistic "I versus
them" mind-set, then the book of Revelation is a classic mythic articulation of just how violent that mind-set and worldview can become.
When we fail to use our angelic potential to move out of I-It consciousness and toward the more inclusive and compassionate realms
of I-Thou and I-I, we find ourselves mired in paranoia, fearing that
anyone who is different from us must therefore be against us.

The fact that Revelation holds out the promise that in the end
God will defeat Satan, that the I-I will at last and for all time overcome the misdirected I-It, demonstrates the unsinkable power of
hope at the heart of humankind.

• • •

Justin Martyr (ca. 110–ca. 165), a pagan philosopher who converted
to Christianity and became a passionate evangelist for his new faith,
attributed all evil to demons, and claimed that those who persecute
Christians were in fact under the influence of demons. These
demons were, in Justin's thinking, the offspring of the sons of God
and the daughters of men mentioned in Genesis. He declared the
gods of the non-Judeo-Christian world to be demons as well.

This was pure innovation on Justin's part. While one can find inklings of this kind of thinking in Hellenistic writing, nowhere in Jewish thought do the rabbis equate the gods of others with demons. That is not to say the rabbis gave any credence to foreign gods. On the contrary, they believed that such gods were figments of the imagination, and had no reality in and of themselves. Justin's position on the other hand allows these gods a level of reality Judaism denies them.

Septimius Tertullian (ca. 160–ca. 230), also a convert to Christianity, was even more outspoken about Satan than was Justin Martyr. Tertullian believed that human beings "call on Satan, the demon chief, in their execrations, as though from some instinctive soul-knowledge of him . . . We are instructed, moreover, by our sacred books how from certain angels who fell of their own free will, there sprang a more wicked demon-brood, condemned of God along with the authors of their race, and that chief demon we have referred to."[13]

We can see where this is going. If humans naturally call upon Satan, and only the followers of Christ are free from this, then all who are not Christians are almost by definition Satanists. And, if Satanism is indeed innate, arising naturally from the body, then perhaps the body itself is evil.

The emerging dualism in the Church, pitting the spiritual against the material, the Lord of Light against the Lord of Darkness, is already given clear articulation in the *Epistle of Barnabas*, a first-century Christian text.

Barnabas speaks of the "Black One" who dominates the world. "There are two ways of teaching and power, one of light and one of darkness . . . over the one are set light-bringing angels of God, but over the other angels of Satan. And the one is Lord from eternity to eternity, and the other is the ruler of the present time of iniquity."[14]

The idea that Satan rules this world and this time, meaning that Satan is the God of time and space, is problematic in any monotheistic faith. Irenaeus, another second-century Christian scholar, sought to make sense of this dualism by linking it to Adam's fall. He believed that it was the fall of Adam that brought humanity under the subjugation of Satan and, at the same time, robbed human beings of their immortality. Jesus reversed the process: "The death of Jesus contributed to man's salvation in three ways. It was at once the crowning act of obedience, a recapitulation of Adam's fall, and the payment of a price to Satan in return for man's release."[15]

This last notion is startling. The idea that Jesus's death was a ransom goes back to the early Jewish understanding of atonement: the death of an animal atones for one's sins. That is to say, one is held hostage by one's sins, and the death of the animal is the ransom one must pay for one's release from that bondage. The death of Jesus was seen by these early Christian writers as the ultimate atonement for the sins of humanity. But with Irenaeus we find that we are held hostage not to sin but to Satan, and that it was Satan and not God who was pacified by Jesus's death. In his view God was obligated to pay a ransom to Satan, and the death of his Son, Jesus, was the agreed-upon sum. This elevation of Satan from the role of God's "prosecutor" and loyal voice of opposition found in the book of Job to the rebellious and autonomous enemy of God marked a clear shift in thinking. And the fact that it was this dualistic notion that triumphed in Christianity suggests that it marked a clear shift in human consciousness as well.

The book of Genesis itself makes it clear that creation is intrinsically good (Genesis 1:31). While the disobedience of Adam and Eve has grave consequences for both the First Couple *and* their descendants, it does not in any way change God's assessment of creation itself—it is still "very good." As Christian thinking evolved and the notion that the world had been given over to Satan became the norm, the very notion of creation's intrinsic goodness and value was lost. This world became Satan's kingdom rather than God's, and the only hope was to escape this world for the next, with souls intact and secure in the faith in the ransom of Christ.

. . .

In Islam the Arabic word for Satan, *shaytan*, means "adversary," as it does in Hebrew. The term in Arabic can refer to both a singular character called Satan or to a category of demonic beings. Among these, one in particular, called *Iblis,* is often taken to be synonymous with Shaytan, and like the Christian Satan, becomes an independent rebel against God.

Shaytan/Iblis was a disobedient angel exiled from heaven. The reason for his exile is his refusal to bow before Adam. For this act of disobedience Iblis is called a "stoned devil," and becomes the sworn enemy of humankind. "Remember, when We asked the angels to bow in homage to Adam, they all bowed but Iblis, who disdained and turned insolent, and so became a disbeliever" (Qur'an 2:34).[16]

According to Abu Jafar Muhammad ibn Jarir al-Tabari (d. 932), an early Muslim historian and jurist,

> God had made [Iblis] beautiful and refined him and enthroned him over the lower heavens and earth. His name was Iblis. He made him one of the treasures of Paradise, but he was puffed up with pride against his

master, claimed the supreme authority, and summoned all who were before him to worship him. And God transformed him into a stoned devil, and made him ugly and stripped from him what he had granted him and cursed him and drove him from heaven immediately, together with his adherents, to the fire of hell.[17]

Iblis was the leader of a tribe of spiritual beings called the *jinn*. In Islamic and pre-Islamic folklore the jinn are spirits created out of fire who share with humanity the capacity for good and evil. Jinn are less righteous than humans and less physical. They rarely appear in human form, and Iblis especially often acts in ways that make it difficult to separate him from the angels.

• • •

Very different from the older Jewish concept of Satan, the Christian and Islamic accounts of the Devil share some common themes. They both turn the Devil into a powerful player in the cosmic battle between good and evil, they both argue that the Devil was originally an angel in God's court who became Satan/Shaytan, the adversary, because of an act of disobedience, and they both pit the Devil against humanity, and have the Devil blame humanity for his fall from heaven.

Christian dualism did have its limits, however: Satan was created by God, and will ultimately be defeated by God. In this way Christian dualists, like the earlier Zoroastrians who held a similar belief, managed to maintain their claim to be monotheists. Nevertheless, the need to free God from impurity and evil persisted. The notion that God is all-good, all-loving, and all-compassionate marked a psycho-spiritual split in human consciousness that gave rise to grave consequences and fundamental questions: Once we have identified all good with God, what are we to do with the evil we face daily? If God is all-loving and all-compassionate, how do we explain the evil that befalls good people? This is the challenge of theodicy: why does God permit bad things to happen to good people?

The simplest answer is that it is all part of God's plan. Since God's plan is beyond the understanding of human beings there is no need to inquire any further. Simply trust that God knows what God is doing. While this may be comforting, it does nothing to address the real challenge posed by the belief in an all-loving God—what to do with evil.

The Devil symbolizes the dark side of the human personality. It is the devil we know because it is the devil we are. It is everything we are that we wish we were not. As long as we admit that we have a dark side, we have the potential to tame it. But most people do not admit this, and project their devil onto others.

With the splitting of God into a Good God and an evil Anti-God, Light and Dark, the Lord and Satan, came the splitting of humanity into good and evil, the beloved and the despised, the saved and the damned. To be on the side of God was to be free from the darkness. Since this is in fact impossible (light and dark go together like front and back, left and right), the only way the illusion of being free of the dark can be maintained is to spend an extraordinary amount of energy denying one's dark side—while projecting it onto others. The saved need the damned. In fact the saved need the damned more than they need the Savior. This is why the role of Satan became so powerful in Christianity.

The more we identify with the Lord of Light the more we must stand against the Lord of Darkness and those who support him. In practice this turns out to be anyone who we feel stands in the way of our achieving our desires. Since we are on God's side, we are free of the devil; hence, whatever we desire must be what God desires as well, and thus anyone who seeks to thwart that desire must be seeking to thwart God. The logic is flawless. But the assumption that light and darkness can be separated is false.

We cannot escape our devil. The best we can do is to take ownership of it. In rabbinic Judaism the dark side is called the *Yetzer ha-Rah*, the Inclination for Evil. The *Yetzer ha-Rah* is our inclination for self-preservation taken to extremes, is selfishness run rampant. It is the ego-centered consciousness gone astray, open to evil when we seek to achieve ego-centered aims using wicked means.

What keeps the *Yetzer ha-Rah* in check? The *Yetzer ha-Tov*, the Inclination for Good. In the book of Deuteronomy there is the command to love God "with all your heart" (Deuteronomy 6:5). The rabbis understood this to refer to both inclinations, the Good and the Evil (*Sifrei Deuteronomy* 32). They further taught that selfishness arrives at birth. It is this capacity for self-preservation and self-development that is the focus of the first twelve years of life. With the teenage years, however, the natural capacity for self-care is coupled with *Yetzer ha-Tov*, the capacity to selflessly care for others. It is then that one can love God with all one's heart by using the *Yetzer ha-Tov* to guide the *Yetzer ha-Rah* toward actions that serve both self and others.

In other words, as the Christian writers were expanding the battle between good and evil into a cosmic struggle between God and Satan, the rabbis were restricting it to a psychological battle within each human being. This is nowhere made more clear than in a midrash reflecting on Jacob's Dream, "And he dreamt: And a ladder was set on the earth with its top reaching into the heavens, and angels of God were ascending and descending on it" (Genesis 28:12). According to this midrash, Rabbi Hiyya the Elder and Rabbi Jannai argued over the meaning of Jacob's vision. Hiyya said the angels were ascending and descending upon the ladder, and Jannai believed they were ascending and descending upon Jacob. Hiyya's position requires no additional interpretation, but Jannai's position means that the ascending angels were exalting Jacob and the descending angels were degrading him (*Genesis Rabbah* 68:12).

The key to the argument between Rabbi Hiyya and Rabbi Jannai rests with their respective understanding of the Hebrew pronoun *hu*, which can mean both "it" and "him." If *hu* refers to "it," then Rabbi Hiyya is correct and the angels were ascending and descending on the ladder. But if *hu* refers to "him," to Jacob, then Rabbi Jannai is right and the angels are either supporting or denigrating Jacob. In our understanding of angels it is Rabbi Jannai's explanation that makes the most sense: there are angels (angelic potential) that can denigrate us, by supporting our capacity for evil; and there are angels (angelic potential) that can praise us, by supporting our capacity for good. In this sense we can imagine the descending angels as pushing Jacob down to his *Yetzer ha-Rah*, the inclination for evil, and the ascending angels as lifting him up to his *Yetzer ha-Tov*, the inclination for good.

But it is not always easy to tell which angels are which. If we take Rabbi Jannai literally and imagine that the angels are verbally denigrating and praising, we have to realize that the angels supportive of the *Yetzer ha-Rah* will praise us when we do evil, and the angels of the *Yetzer ha-Tov* will damn us when we do evil. And vice versa. Not the praise itself matters, but *what* the angels are praising.

This leads to the need for a great deal of humility on our part. We have to be able to look beyond mere praise and denigration to understand what motivates both—what is being praised and what is being condemned. In our reading of the angelic capacity it is our motivation and intent that matter most.

What then shall we do with the evil of which we are capable? Reb Nachman of Breslov, a nineteenth-century Jewish sage, saw the answer to this question in the command to "love your neighbor as yourself" (Leviticus 19:18). While the plain meaning of the text is clear—one should treat others with love and respect—Reb Nachman saw another meaning in it as well. The Hebrew phrase *ray-ah-cha*, "your neighbor," could (given the fact that the Hebrew Bible is written without vowels) also be read as *rah-ah-cha*, "your evil." We should come to accept our dark side as part of our selves, no less part of our selves than our light or good side.

Accepting our dark side, of course, doesn't mean excusing it or acquiescing to it. It is our obligation to control our capacity for evil, and to channel its energies toward the good, but to do so we must first admit that we have a dark side and then embrace it as a part of our nature. This is what Reb Nachman is challenging us to do. By "loving our evil" we are embracing our dark side rather than denying or rejecting it. A rejected or denied *rah* allows our capacity for evil to continue unchecked, while embracing the dark side allows us to engage its energies in a manner that minimizes the damage it can do.

Six

The Angel of Death

Ͼϖ〜ϛϡ

THE HEBREW BIBLE mentions "destroying angels" in Exodus (12:23), 2 Samuel (24:16), and Isaiah (37:36), a grim reaper in Jeremiah (9:20), and angry "messengers of death" in Proverbs (16:14), but none of these are personified as the angel of death.

The angel of death develops in the postbiblical literature of the Apocrypha. The *Book of Tobit* (3:8, 3:17), for example, names Asmodeus as the angel of death, while the Talmud sometimes uses an etymologically similar name, Ashmedai. Scholars believe that both names have a Zoroastrian influence. In the Avestan language of Zoroaster we find *Daeva Aesma* as the demon (daeva) of wrath (aesma).[1]

In addition to Ashmedai, the Talmud also uses the name *Mal'akh haMavet* (the messenger/angel of death) and identifies him with Satan and the *Yetzer ha-Rah*, the human inclination toward selfishness and evil (*Bava Batra* 16a). According to the Talmud, the only reason Israel accepted the Torah was to secure an antidote to the permanence of death (*Avodah Zarah*, 5a). Despite the linking of the angel of death with Satan in a single Talmudic passage, *Mal'akh haMavet* is, as his name implies, a messenger of God and not the enemy of God that Satan becomes in later Christian texts.

Samael is often seen as synonymous with the angel of death. Samael is mentioned in a number of places, though which of these was first is hard to say. *Pirkei de-Rabbi Eliezer* links Samael to the sin of Adam, *Exodus Rabbah* 21:7 tells us that Samael argued against the redemption of the children of Israel from Egyptian slavery, and *Deuteronomy Rabbah* names Samael as the angel sent to take the soul of Moses.

Most of what we know about the angel of death in Judaism comes from the rabbis, especially those rabbis engaged in midrashic imagination.

One question that concerned both the midrashists and the much earlier writer of Genesis is how death came into the world. The Genesis writer tells us that it is a punishment from God for Adam and Eve's eating from the Tree of Knowledge of Good and Evil. The midrashist has a different story:

> Prior to their leaving Eden Eve encountered Samael
> (the angel of death) and his son who were also enjoy-
> ing a walk in the Garden. The angel approached Eve
> and asked her to keep an eye on the boy while Samael

ran an errand. Eve agreed, and as soon as Samael departed the boy began to howl and scream inconsolably.

Adam came upon Eve and the child, and demanded that the boy stop crying. The more Adam demanded silence the louder the boy's cries became. Enraged Adam grabbed the boy and struck him dead. Yet even in death the boy kept screaming. Beside himself with anger, Adam then chopped the corpse into small pieces, but that too failed to silence the boy. Fearful of what may befall him for killing the boy, Adam cooked the remains and, in a horrible reversed foreshadowing of what was to happen at the Tree of Knowledge, ate of the remains and fed some to Eve. When they had finished eating, Samael returned and asked about the welfare of his son. Adam and Eve denied ever seeing the boy.

Suddenly the voice of the child spoke from within the hearts of both Adam and Eve saying, "There is nothing you can do here, Father. Go. Depart. I have penetrated into the heart of these humans and will inhabit them and the hearts of their children until the end of time."[2]

It is not hard to see the link between the Genesis myth and this midrash. Indeed, the midrash is a fantastical riff on the earlier Genesis theme of eating. In the older story Adam and Eve ate a fruit, and the consequence of their doing so was death. In the midrash they eat death itself.

Evidently, death is brought into the world through misdirected human consumption. When we eat what we should not eat we die. Not right away, of course, but eventually. This speaks directly to the angst of the ego-centered mind. Living with a belief rooted in I-It consciousness that sees the world as something to be exploited for one's own benefit, the "I" consumes the world around it—the "It." We become like the giants who devour the earth in the midrash associated with the Genesis myth (Genesis 6:4) of the coupling of the angels with human females. That is to say, we take our angelic faculty, our potential to see the world in larger and more integrated ways, and use it not to embrace this larger world, but to devour it instead; use it not to realize our place in the larger life of I-Thou and I-I, but instead to seek to usurp that larger life, to swallow it up.

• • •

Elsewhere in rabbinic literature we learn that the angel of death was created by God on the first day of creation, making it clear that death is a part of life and not its enemy (*Midrash Tanhuma* on Genesis 39:1). And we are told that at the hour of our death the angel stands at our head with a raised sword to which clings a single poisonous drop. When we see the angel we are startled and our mouth opens, at which point the angel shakes the drop into our mouth causing us to turn yellow and die (*Avodah Zarah*, 20b).

It may be this teaching regarding the poisonous drop that gave rise to the following midrash of King David and the angel of death. Here, too, we encounter the image of death entering through the mouth, warning us about the dual nature of consumption—it can both support life and destroy it:

The King inquired of God as to the day of his death. God explained that such knowledge was not to be given to humans, even such a righteous one as David. David then asked God to tell him on which day of the week he was to die, and God revealed to David that he would die on a Saturday, the Jewish Sabbath.

From that day forth, David spent every Sabbath steeped in the study of Torah, hoping in this way to protect himself from the Angel of Death. When the Sabbath of his death arrived, the Angel of Death found the King poring over the Torah. So immersed was he in his studies that the Angel could find no way to take his soul. The Angel had to find a way to distract David.

Not far from where David was studying, the King had built a beautiful garden. The Angel of Death entered the garden and began to shake the trees violently. David heard the noise and went out into the garden to see who was in the trees. Yet even as he grabbed a ladder and began to climb a tree to investigate he continued to ponder the words of Torah and the Angel of Death could not touch him.

As he reached a high rung, the Angel caused the next rung to break beneath David's weight and the King fell hard to the ground. Stunned by the fall, David ceased to recite the words of Torah, and his mouth fell open. It was then that the Angel of Death took David's soul to Paradise.[3]

King David is not the first leader of Israel whose soul could not be taken easily by Samael, the angel of death. Samael struggled greatly with Moses, too, according to the midrash.

After Moses led his people Israel for forty years, his life was at an end and the time of his death had drawn near. God called to the angel Gabriel ordering him to fetch Moses's soul and bring it to God. But Gabriel refused saying, "I would not presume to take the soul of such a spiritual man as Moses." God then demanded that Michael fetch Moses's soul, but he too refused arguing as did Gabriel that Moses was too holy for even an angel to take his soul.

God then turned to the angel Zagzagel who had been Moses's teacher, but he too refused saying it was not fitting that the teacher take the life of the student.

No one would take the soul of Moses and it looked like Moses would not die after all. Then Samael came before the Throne of God and said, "Is this one, Moses, greater than the first one, Adam? Is he different from Abraham or Jacob or the fathers of the twelve tribes? I took the souls of each of these, so permit me to do the same for Moses."

God said to Samael, "Moses is greater than all of these. How would you approach him? If you sought to take his soul through his face, you would fail for you cannot look upon his face anymore than you can look upon My Face. If you would take it from his hands, you would fail, for those hands held the Torah. If you would take it from his feet, you would fail, for his feet have walked the paths of Heaven. How will you take it from him?"

Samael said, "I do not know, but I will find a way." And God gave him His consent.

Samael found Moses engaged in writing the Name of God. Samael drew his sword and summoned all the anger that was in him hoping in this way to frighten Moses and find a way to his soul through his fear. Moses saw the angel flying toward him and looked him in the eye, whereupon Samael went blind and doubled over in pain.

Moses said to him, "Leave me or I will cut off your head!"

"Be not angry with me, Moses," Samael replied still blind and suffering, "God has placed your soul in my hands."

Moses said, "I will not give you my soul," and Samuel fled back to God in terror.

God was furious with Samael: "Bring me the soul of Moses!"

"I cannot! His power is greater than I can breach!"

"You were so eager to kill Moses and now you stand before Me humiliated. Is this what we shall remember of Samael?"

Samael drew upon his shame and humiliation and mustered a fury unlike even he had known before. Drawing his sword he flew enraged at Moses, but the prophet drew his staff engraved with the Name of God and did battle with Samael, forcing the angel to flee in defeat. Moses raced after him and tripped him with his staff and blinded him with the light of his face. Moses was about to kill the Angel of Death when God called to him from Heaven, "Moses, spare him for the world still has need of his services."

Then God said to Moses, "Why do you struggle on? Your death is at hand."

"Lord," Moses said, "You have honored me with so much, please do not now give my soul over to the defeated Samael."

"This I grant you, Moses," God said. "I Myself will come for you."

God descended to earth accompanied by three angels, Michael, Gabriel, and Zagzagel. Gabriel arranged a bed on which Moses could rest. Michael spread over him a purple blanket, and Zagzagel placed a woolen pillow beneath Moses's head. Michael then stood by Moses's right side, while Gabriel stood by his left and Zagzagel by his feet. God then said to Moses, "Cross your feet," and he did so. "Lay your arms across your chest," and he did so. "Close your eyes," and he did so.

God then spoke directly to Moses's soul saying, "My daughter, the one hundred and twenty years allotted to this body are up and you must relinquish it." Moses's soul replied, "I have grown to love this man, Lord, for his righteousness is only surpassed by his humility. Please do not suffer me to leave him."

And God said, "You shall dwell under the Throne of Glory."

But Moses's soul continued to entreat God saying, "Remember how you suspended the angels Azza and Azazel between heaven and earth for their love of the daughters of men? Allow me to remain suspended as well for my love of this son of a woman."

When Moses realized his soul would not leave him he said to her, "My soul, is my death a victory for Samael?"

"No," she said, "I will go into God's hands not Samael's."

"Will you cry over my death as will the Israelites?"

"No," she said, "I am beyond tears."

"Will you suffer the fires of Hell when I die?"

"No," she said, "I will dwell in the highest Heaven."

"Then let us be done with it," Moses said, and asked his soul to go to God.

And God bent down and kissed Moses on the mouth and inhaled the breath of life from Moses as He had once exhaled it into Adam. God then buried Moses in a grave whose whereabouts is still unknown. All that is known is this: A tunnel connects the grave of Moses with those of the Patriarchs, and the body of Moses is as fresh today as the day God laid it to rest.[4]

We can see both a parallel and a difference between death entering through the mouth in the midrashim of Adam and Eve, and King David, and the Kiss of God here that is also the Kiss of Death for Moses. All three myths link death to the mouth, but in the case of Moses God takes out life rather than puts in death. God takes *back* from Moses the *ruach*, the breath that he breathed *into* Adam in Genesis.

God as we understand God in this book is the I-I, the Source and Substance of all reality. In Genesis God pours his breath into Adam the way we might say the ocean pours itself into a wave. The breath of God is the I-I taking up residence in the human as the I-Thou and the I-It. As we reverse the process, and move from ego-centered mind to world-centered soul, and finally into God-centered spirit we are, in a sense, returning the *ruach* to God, and returning ourselves to our source.

• • •

While King David eventually succumbs to death in the rabbinic midrash, his descendant Jesus defeats death in the New Testament. In the book of Acts, for example, we learn that death could not hold Jesus: "But God raised him up, having freed him from death, because it was impossible for him to be held in its power" (Acts 2:24).

In Paul's letter to the Romans we learn that "death exercised dominion from Adam to Moses" (Romans 5:14), but that Jesus and those who believe in him as Christ are free from the eternality of death (Romans 6:3–11). The second letter to Timothy says that Jesus "abolished death" (2 Timothy 1:10), and in the first letter to the Corinthians Paul writes that though "the last enemy to be destroyed is death" (1 Corinthians 15:26), the final end of death will indeed come.

None of these examples in the New Testament, however, speaks of an angel of death. For this we need to turn once more to the book of

Revelation: "I looked and there was a pale green horse! Its rider's name was Death, and Hades followed with him; they were given authority over a fourth of the earth, to kill with sword, famine, and pestilence, and by the wild animals of the earth" (Revelation 6:8).

It is clear that Death in Revelation is a servant of God, for his authority to slaughter one quarter of the earth was "given" to him by God. Death is clearly not Satan who, in Revelation, is the cosmic and independent enemy of God. When the task of Death and Hades is done, and the final Day of Judgment arrives, death itself dies: "And the sea gave up the dead that were in it, Death and Hades gave up the dead that were in them, and all were judged according to what they had done. Then Death and Hades were thrown into the lake of fire. This is the second death, the lake of fire" (Revelation 20:13–14).

Death as something to be defeated is alien to Islam, which looks upon death more positively as liberation from the suffering of life, and a transition to eternal life with Allah. The Qur'an tells us: "Say: 'The angel of death appointed over you will take away your soul, then you will be sent back to your Lord'" (Qur'an 32:11).[5] The angel is unnamed but thought to be 'Izra'il. Overall not much is known of the angel of death from either the Qur'an or the Hadith, and little distinguishes him from the other angels of Islam.

• • •

Perhaps in Hinduism a comparable figure to the angel of death in the West is *Yama* or *Yamaraj*, the Lord of Death. Yamaraj is often depicted riding a black buffalo and carrying a rope lasso that he uses to bring the souls of the dead to his realm called *Yamalok*. In Yamalok, Yamaraj consults the records kept on each being's life and decides that being's fate in the next incarnation.

One of the most interesting myths regarding Yama is found in the *Legend of Gokarnatirtha*:[6]

> In Mathura, a holy city in the state of Uttar Pradesh, there lived two men, one young and the other old, both of whom were named Gokarna. It was time for the older Gokarna to die and Yama send his agents to bring the old man to him. By mistake they took the younger Gokarna to Yama instead. Realizing the error, Yama ordered the young man back to life, but he refused.
>
> Yama then sought to bribe the man. In exchange for Yama granting the wrongly deceased Gokarna a single request, the young man would allow himself to be returned to life on earth. The younger Gokarna agreed and asked Yama to explain to him the nature of hell, and how one can avoid going there. Yama told him in detail the twenty-one hells and the unrepented evil deeds that cause one to be reborn in one of them.
>
> Meanwhile the agents of Yama had returned to earth and taken the soul of the older Gokarna to Yama, but seeing as how the younger Gokarna was still with Yama, the older man was allowed to live and return to earth. By the time Yama had finished speaking with the younger Gokarna and returning him to earth, both Gorkanas were alive and well.
>
> It so happened that the two Gokarnas met, and the younger explained what had happened to the older. Both men then became devote, did penance for all

their misdeeds, and when Yama sent for them again both were reborn in heaven.

• • •

The angel of death symbolizes the capacity for human transformation, moving from ego-centered mind toward God-centered spirit. This feels like death to the former, though it proves to be just the opposite once the transformation is complete. In this sense, of course, the death we are talking about is not so much physical as psycho-spiritual. The ego-centered mind must, as the Sufis say, "die before you die." That is, the I-It must die to its illusion of exclusivity and reawaken to the reality of the all-embracing I-I nonduality.

This notion of "dying before you die" is powerfully symbolized by the ascension of humans to heaven. We can find two types of ascension myths. In the first, the ascending human remains in heaven; in the second, he or she returns to earth to be of further service to humanity.

Seven

The Ascended Ones

კარა

INTERTWINED WITH ANGEL myths are the myths about the ascended ones: these are not angels who descend to earth disguised as humans, but humans who ascend to heaven and become messengers of God. These are women and men who become vehicles for the divine, both those who ascend and remain in heaven and those who ascend and return to earth.

Of these two ways of ascending the second is the more interesting to us, because these distinctive individuals have reached the state of God-centered spirit and are able to see all realms and all beings as manifestations of the One. It is this insight that allows them to take on ego-centered mind without being trapped in it.

But first we will look at the transformation of the human Enoch into the angel Metatron, a classic example of a human being who ascends and becomes totally transformed by the divine, to the point where returning to earth as a human and taking on ego-centered mind is no longer possible.

Enoch/Metatron

We have already examined Enoch's first-person account of his meeting with the archangel Raphael. Now we will encounter him not as he saw himself, but as others came to see him over time. Enoch became in the minds of Jews not only a human who conversed with angels, but a human who became the most powerful angel of all, Metatron, the Lesser YHVH.

Enoch was the son of Jared whose worship of angels and nature, according to the ancient rabbis, began the spiritual degradation of humankind. While there is no biblical reference for this, *yared* in Hebrew means "to descend," and this may have been the rabbis' way of explaining why he bore that name.

Enoch, however, rejected the ways of his father and "walked with God" (Genesis 5:24). While his father continued to live and sire children for another eight hundred years, Enoch seems to have had nothing to do with him. When Enoch himself reached the age of sixty-five he fathered Methuselah, and then continued to walk with God for another three hundred years. It was then that something unusual happened: "and he was not, for God took him" (Genesis 5:24).

The Bible makes it very clear that the human life span in those days was centuries longer than that of Enoch. In effect the 365-year-old Enoch died in early middle age. Yet to say he died at all is to read more into the text than the Bible allows. The Bible does not say that

Enoch died, only that God took him. To understand why and what took place we turn to the midrash.

The answer to what happened to Enoch was linked to a book, *Sefer Raziel*,[1] meaning "The Book of the Angel Raziel." *Raziel* means "Secret of God," and the book was said to contain all knowledge, both material and spiritual.[2] According to *Targum Ecclesiastes* (10, 20), an early but undated collection of midrash woven from the book of Ecclesiastes, the angel Raziel stood on the peak of Mount Horeb every day and shouted out these secrets to all humankind. Clearly the Secret of God was something God wanted humanity to know, and Raziel was the means to accomplish that. To make sure this wisdom was not lost, the angel placed it in a book and gave the book to Adam.

When the angels heard that the book had been given to Adam and that Adam's wisdom had blossomed, they grew jealous. They wanted the book for themselves. First a band of angels came and prostrated themselves before Adam hoping in this way to cause him to sin and proclaim himself God. But Adam was not moved by their worship saying, "Do not pray to me, but with me to YHVH."

Having failed to cause Adam to sin, the angels managed to steal the book from him and tossed it into the sea; if they couldn't have it, at least the human would be deprived of the book as well. Adam begged God for help in finding it, and God commanded *Rahab*, the Angel of the Sea, to find the book and restore it to Adam.

To keep the book safe, Adam hid it in a cave, but the whereabouts of the cave was forgotten when Adam died. For centuries the book was lost, but God sent a dream to Enoch showing him the cave and commanding him to find and study *Sefer Raziel*. Enoch committed the book to memory, and hid it once again.[3]

The key here is the internalization of the book. Adam read it; Enoch memorized it, that is he *became* it. This is a huge step. The myth is saying that with Enoch knowledge was completely digested. Adam, as we saw, ate from the Tree of Knowledge but could not internalize it. He became *achad*, alienated. Then he ate the son of Samael and became even more cut off and fearful. The knowledge he gleaned from *Sefer Raziel* allowed him to live long, wisely, and well, but it did not transform him in any way. Why? Because he did not "eat" the book, but only read it. The knowledge did not penetrate him and transform him.

Enoch on the other hand internalized the wisdom of Raziel, and it transformed him completely, removing him from the earthly plane and taking him bodily into heaven. This again contrasts Adam's experience. Adam was exiled from the Garden; Enoch leaves earth. Adam is cut off from his divine nature; Enoch (as we will see in a moment) loses his humanity. While Enoch is certainly the greater example of human spiritual unfolding, neither he nor Adam complete the circle. Adam does not return to the Garden and Enoch does not return to earth. Completing the circle will have to wait for other humans.

By internalizing *Sefer Raziel* Enoch ascends to heaven and becomes the Witness, the angel Metatron. In *3 Enoch*, a third-century CE text about Rabbi Ishmael ben Elisha's ascension to the Chariot or Throne of God and his encounter with Metatron, it is explained how he was transformed from human into angel under the direction of the archangels Michael and Gabriel:

> Enoch was taken to heaven to serve as witness and to attest to God's justice, despite the destruction decreed against the living. God established a throne for Enoch and let it be known throughout the heavens that from this moment on Enoch would be known as Metatron.
>
> God said, "Henceforth my servant Metatron will reign over all my princes in heaven, only those angels bearing my name are exempt from his rule. Any angel desiring to speak to me will speak to him instead. Metatron will convey my will. Whatever he commands is to be done, but do not worry, for the two angels called Wisdom and Understanding are his advisors. They will make known to him the customs of earth and heaven, and fill him with the knowledge of the present and the future."
>
> The transformation of Enoch into Metatron was fierce: his flesh turned to flame, his bones to glowing coals, his eyes shone with starlight, and his eyeballs became fiery sparks. His entire being was a consuming fire. To his right flames danced, to his left torches gleamed, and all around him swirled gale and tornado, hurricane and thunder.[4]

This is what the angels feared: that a human would rule over them. Not a human in its lowly and alienated state of *achad*, but the fully realized human who has left behind the narrow ego-centered mind and is transformed by God into one who knows the ways of heaven and earth.

Metatron, whose name may come from the Greek *meta*, "beyond," and *thronom*, "the throne [of God]," is, as his name suggests, beyond the throne realm of even the angels and resides just below God in the theological hierarchy of the rabbinic imagination. Metatron is served by the angels of wisdom and understanding, so he himself surpasses these. His is greater than the godlike status promised to Adam and Eve by the serpent if they would eat of the Tree of Knowledge. Enoch/Metatron is immortal not in the sense of living forever in the endless stream of time, which is what eating from the Tree of Life would provide, but in the sense of having transcended time altogether.

Metatron is not an angel only, nor is he only human. He does not die or lose his body. He is not the spirit of Enoch or the soul unbound by the body. Enoch is taken to heaven both body and mind, and turned into fire, pure energy, while yet still maintaining both body and mind.

This myth of Enoch/Metatron is telling us that in some way the human embraces the cosmos. While describing this as a physical encompassing of the cosmos, the myth more likely is pointing to a level of psycho-spiritual awareness—God-centered consciousness— that sees all things as aspects of the divine. This is the I-I awareness that knows the universe as the body of God.

In his new form Enoch grew 72 wings, one for each of the 72 Hebrew Names of God, opened 365,000 eyes that he might see all that happens daily, and was transubstantiated from flesh to pure fire. He was then given a crown similar to that worn by God, and established in a heavenly Temple paralleling the Temple in Jerusalem. This heavenly Temple was called the tabernacle of the *Naar*, literally the Youth, referring to the Lesser YHVH that was *Metatron*, and it was from there that Metatron offered the souls of the righteous as penance for the Jewish people during their exile (*Numbers Rabbah*, 12:12).

According to the *Zohar*, the central text of medieval Jewish mysticism compiled by the Spanish mystic Rabbi Moses de Leon (ca. 1250–1305), Metatron is composed of the heavenly union of God's masculine and feminine aspects (*Zohar* 1:143a, 162a–b). And in later kabbalistic thought Metatron appears as the angel of *devekut*, mystical union with YHVH (*Sefer ha-Hezyanot* 1:23; *Otzer Chayyim* folio 111a).

The *Zohar* says that when Adam sinned and became *achad*, a seemingly alienated self obsessed with its delusion of uniqueness and separation, his capacity to achieve full divine consciousness was removed from him. When Enoch was born that capacity was placed in Enoch instead where it could once again be cultivated:

> Enoch was born just outside the Garden of Eden. From birth a holy light glowed within him, and covered him, and made him the most beautiful of men. Enoch sought out the Tree of Life at the center of the Garden. When he found it he breathed deeply of its aroma, and his heart filled with the spirit of the Tree. Suddenly angels from heaven descended and instructed Enoch in the deepest wisdom of God. They pulled from the Tree a book that had been hidden there, and handed it to Enoch to study. Enoch read the book carefully and found within it the most sublime

paths of God. As he practiced each path the light within him became even more pure. Soon the light was at its most pristine, and it desired to return to heaven from whence it came, to manifest this purity in the very being of Enoch.[5]

Enoch is the promise that we can overcome our human limitations and reclaim our original divine potential. Importantly the light of God began to shine "within Enoch," and the Light of God became "perfect within him." Enoch's transformation is an inner one first. Only when he embodies the Light of God on earth can he become the fire body of Metatron in heaven. Enoch is symbolic of that which each of us can become, and for which all humanity was destined from the very beginning.[6]

Metatron is called "keeper of the keys" to wisdom, and one of these keys is called "the light of discernment."[7] This light allows humans to explore and ultimately to grasp the most sublime mysteries of creation. "Metatron, then, is the aspect of [God's] glory that is depicted as the measurable *anthropos* (human) who sits upon the throne and appears in prophetic visions."[8] He is the "link between the human and the divine."[9]

Isaiah Tishby, the great scholar of Kabbalah, in his three-volume *Wisdom of the Zohar*, put it this way:

> The soul, which is alone the essence of man according to the Zohar, is extracted from the pure radiance of the divine emanation. It is a divine spark that has been inserted into the physical body. The soul descends and assumes a physical form only in order to acquire a special perfection in the terrestrial world

. . . At root, therefore, in his eternal, spiritual essence, man is very near indeed to the divine realm, and his fall and contamination by sin are no more than manifestations of corruption and degeneration occasioned by his temporal, physical existence. The unique man, Enoch, who was able to achieve the ideal, supernal perfection that was indeed destined for the whole of mankind, but taken from them because of Adam's sin, purified himself of the material defects inherent in corporeal existence, and ascended to the highest levels of the angelic hierarchy. Enoch-Metatron symbolizes the culmination of the ascent for which man is destined to strive, and in this refined image perfect man is superior to the angels.[10]

Metatron is a metaphor for what we can become. Hence the Kabbalistic assertion that "Enoch is Metatron,"[11] in other words, that the human is the divine and can reach the divine through the working of the angelic consciousness. Enoch doesn't become something he is not, but realizes that which he truly is—the "Lesser YHVH," as the Talmud puts it (*Yevamot* 16b; *Sanhedrin* 38b).

The myth of Metatron wants us to see that we are born with the capacity to transcend our limited, ego-centered mind toward God-centered spirit. And yet it is our contention that there is an even "higher" level of realization than that of Metatron. Enoch, the Lesser YHVH, becomes fully divine, but *not* fully human. That is to say he transcends the ego-centered mind and the world-centered soul, but does not embrace them, and hence cannot return to and operate within them in service to those humans who have not yet realized their divine nature.

These enlightened humans, those who ascend to heaven but return to earth, can be found in all cultures. In Judaism we have for example Elijah (2 Kings 2:1–12) who, according to the myth, was taken bodily to heaven and who returns to earth to help the needy and the lost. In Christianity there is Mary, the mother of Jesus, the revered mediator between God and humans. In the Qur'an and Hadith we learn that Muhammad ascended to heaven and returned to earth with wisdom for humankind. And in the Pure Land tradition of Buddhism, Amida Buddha, the Buddha of Infinite Light, in some ways parallels these ascensions, albeit in the mythic language and landscape appropriate to China and Japan.

The ascended ones have completed the journey all humans can take. They began as ego-centered minds. They met angels (meaning they unfolded their angelic potential), transcended the ego-centered realm, and entered the realm of world-centered soul. They then internalized this realm and rose even higher (or dived even deeper) into the God-centered realm of the spirit. Here they became fully God-realized human beings who completely integrated the human and the divine in themselves, and who could then return to earth to help others attempt the same.

The Ascension of Elijah

In the ninth century BCE the united kingdom of David and Solomon split in two, Israel to the north and Judah to the south. Elijah appears in the Bible in 1 Kings 17:1 as a prophet of the northern kingdom. The Bible tells us nothing of his background, but of his ascension (2 Kings 2:1–12) it is quite clear. Here is what happened:

As Elijah and his protégé Elisha traveled from Gilgal toward Bethel, YHVH planned to send a tornado to lift Elijah to heaven. Elijah intended to travel to Bethel alone, but Elisha would not leave him, and as they approached the city other prophets joined them. Pulling Elisha aside they said to him, "Are you aware that today is the day YHVH will take Elijah from you?" Elisha replied, "Yes, I know, but keep silent."

Elijah again sought to separate from Elisha, urging him to wait in Bethel while Elijah would walk on to Jericho, and again Elisha refused to abandon his master. As the two men drew near to Jericho the city's prophets pulled Elisha aside and told him of Elijah's fate. For the second time Elisha replied, "Yes, I know, but keep silent."

For a third time Elijah sought to separate from Elisha, this time telling him he must walk on to the river Jordan, and for a third time his student stayed by his side. When the two men came to the Jordan fifty prophets gathered to see how they would cross.

Elijah took his cloak, rolled it into a tight tube, and struck the water. The river split in two where struck, and Elijah and Elisha walked across on the now dry riverbed.

On the far bank of the Jordan Elijah said to Elisha, "I will soon be taken from you, tell me what I can offer you before I go."

"Please master," Elisha said, "I desire a double portion of your spirit."

"This is a difficult thing, Elisha," Elijah responded,
"but if God allows you to see me rise into heaven, then
what you desire will be granted to you. But if you see
nothing, you will inherit nothing."

The two men continued to talk as they journeyed
toward the Jordan. Suddenly a chariot of fire pulled by
horses of flame raced between the two men, separating
them. A great wind followed the chariot and scooped
Elijah up into the sky.

"Father! Father!" Elisha cried as he watched Elijah
disappear into the heavens, "the chariots of Israel and
its horsemen!"

When Elijah was completely out of sight and
Elisha was certain he would see him no more, Elisha
grabbed his robe and tore it in two as a sign of his
grief and his loss.

It is clear that Elijah knows he is to be taken up into heaven, and
it is equally clear that he wants there to be no witnesses. He tries several times to leave his student Elisha behind, but Elisha will have
none of it. Elisha knows he is to take Elijah's place as a prophet, but
he fears that his spirit is not up to the task, so he asks that Elijah
bestow his own spirit of prophecy upon him twofold. Elijah agrees,
but does nothing specific to make this happen. On the contrary,
Elisha will receive the spirit of his teacher if, and only if, he can witness the ascension of Elijah. That is to say, achieving the capacity to
witness the ascension is itself the reception of the prophetic spirit.

What does this mean? The human ascension to heaven is the
mythopoetic way of speaking of transformation from the ego-

centered mind toward the God-centered spirit. Elisha himself is not ready to make this journey, but he is ready (or so he and Elijah hope) to at least witness such an act and therefore attest to its possibility.

Elisha sees Elijah taken bodily into heaven, suggesting that the transformation includes the body *and* the ego-centered mind that is linked to it. We are not dealing with a dualistic, Gnostic, or antimaterial ideal here. We are being introduced to the fact that the I-I of God includes the I-It of mind and the I-Thou of soul.

And what does the ascended Elijah do? He returns to earth over and over again to lead us mere humans to the truth of our full humanity: "I call upon heaven and earth to witness that whether it be a Jew or a gentile, whether it be a man or a woman, a butler or a maid, the holy spirit will suffuse each of them in keeping with the deeds he or she performs."[12]

In the Jewish tradition Elijah appears in many guises to aid and guide those who are struggling, especially the poor. He was thought to have been the teacher of many early rabbis, and it is said that he will herald the coming of the Messiah: "Lo, I will send the prophet Elijah to you before the coming of the awesome, fearful day of the Lord" (Malachi 3:23). And it is Elijah who visits every Jewish home during the Passover seder to share a bit of wine with the celebrants, and to affirm that some day he will announce the coming of the Messiah and the ending of all oppression and injustice:

> When he [Elijah] ascended on high, he acquired the power of spirituality as an angel indeed, to ascend and to become [afterwards] corporeal and descend to this lower world where you are existing. This is in order to perform miracles or to disclose My power in the world.

He [Elijah] is causing the descent of My power in the
world, forcefully and compellingly, from My great
Name [YHVH], that is an integral part of him. And
because of this great secret he did not have to taste
death, so that he will be able to cause the descent of
My power and disclose My secret by the power of My
precious Name . . . And My power is bound to him and
he is bound to your souls and discloses to you the
secrets of My Torah, without speech. And a time will
come, very soon, that he will reveal himself to you in
body and in spirit, and this will be a sign for the coming of the Messiah. And by his descending to earth
together with him then will he reveal in body and in
spirit, and many others will see him.[13]

Elijah's ascent to heaven is an apotheosis, a transformation of the
human into the fully human and divine. His return to earth is not a
return to ordinary human existence but a breaking into the human
dimension by the divine, a theophany. Elijah becomes a messenger, a
way the divine manifests in the human dimension in order to guide
humans into the divine dimension. Angels play the same role, of
course, and because they do we can be all the more certain of their
metaphoric meaning as faculties for human spiritual transformation.
It is not that Elijah and the other ascended ones become something
they were not, but that they become fully what they, and we, can be.

The Ascension of Isaiah

Unlike some of the other ascension myths we are looking at, the
ascension of Isaiah is clearly experienced by the prophet as a vision

rather than a bodily ascent. One of the major Hebrew prophets, Isaiah began his prophetic life shortly before the death of the Judean King Uzziah, perhaps in the year 740 or 742 BCE, and continued to prophesy for over four decades. The book of Isaiah purports to be an autobiographical account of the prophet's career. Here is Isaiah's account of his vision of heaven:

> During the year of King Uzziah's death, I saw YHVH sitting on a throne, high and towering, its legs filling the Temple. Above it stood the seraphim, each with six wings: two covered his face, two covered his feet, and two he used to fly. Each angel cried to the others saying, "Holy, holy, holy, is YHVH, master of multitudes; the whole earth teems with his splendor." The doorposts quaked from the sound of their calling, and the Temple filled with smoke. I said: "Woe is me! I am doomed, for I am a man of unclean lips, and I live among a people of unclean lips; yet my eyes have seen YHVH, the Master of Legions!"
>
> Then one of the seraphs flew to me, holding a live coal taken with a pair of tongs from atop the altar. The seraph touched it to my mouth saying, "Now that this has touched your lips, your guilt has departed and your sin is erased." Suddenly I heard YHVH asking, "Whom could I send to represent Us?" and I responded, "Here! Send me!" (Isaiah 6:1–8)

Isaiah did not seek this vision. He is clear that he has no place in heaven for he is of unclean lips. Why is it that unclean lips make him unfit for heaven? What does this phrase "unclean lips" really mean?

The obvious answer is that it refers to impiety of speech. Yet nowhere in the Bible do we find Isaiah speaking falsely, and, by the time we come to this vision, the prophet has already spoken for five chapters. Are we to discount his words prior to this vision? Of course not; something else must be meant.

The answer is found in the very nature of speech: it requires a speaker. The very act of speaking implies there is someone doing the speaking. Talk creates the talker. This is true of words spoken aloud and words spoken in the privacy of our own minds. We cannot think without words, and the words coupled with the act of thinking produces the idea of a thinker, a self, an ego, an *achad* separate from the whole of life. What Isaiah is saying is this: "Woe is me, for the ego I am cannot survive in the nonduality of heaven. I will be devoured by the Truth of my own illusory nature."

It is then, when Isaiah's ego-centered mind is in great distress, that the angel approaches him with a burning coal from the altar of God. He presses the coal to Isaiah's lips and the sin of ego-centrism is ended—his guilt departs and his sin is blotted out. What an interesting notion: *first* the guilt departs, *then* the sin is ended. One would expect the exact opposite: the sin creates the guilt, so end the sin and the guilt too will vanish. Why the reversal?

Isaiah's guilt over his unclean lips is the drama of his own egoism. The more guilty he feels, the more he laments; the more he laments, the more he reinforces the illusion that there is someone lamenting. The very guilt over falling into the delusion of separateness from God keeps the separateness going. So the angel ends the guilt, silences Isaiah's drama, and then the sin, the original delusion that Isaiah is *achad*, not a unique part of God but an alien apart from God, ceases.

To interpret this further, we can assume that the burning coal caused Isaiah great pain. Then only after his moaning ceases, God's question is heard: "Whom could I send to represent Us?" Who now, God asks, understands the Good News of the union of human and divine, and can bring this back to the people that they might change their ways and live out their own divinity? And from his inner silence Isaiah can now respond, "Here! Send me!"

The "I" that Isaiah now knows is not the ego-centered mind of the "I-It," but the much greater God-centered spirit of the "I-I."

The Ascension of Rabbi Ishmael

Rabbi Ishmael ben Elisha (90–135 CE) was one of the early rabbinic sages and Jewish mystics. A deeply pious man, Rabbi Ishmael was renowned both for his intimacy with God and his concern with the poor, and he is most famous for providing fine clothing and dowries for penniless young women so that they might find suitable husbands (*Nedarim*, 9:10). He practiced the *Merkavah* or Chariot mysticism popular among rabbis of the first three centuries of the common era. Practitioners sought to imitate the prophet Ezekiel, and induce their own visions of God's Chariot (Throne). Suggestive in regard to our premise, followers of the Merkavah mysticism were called "descenders to the Chariot," perhaps meaning that while the vision was one of ascent, they themselves understood their journey to be an internal voyage of descent into the deepest and most inclusive levels of consciousness.

According to legend, during the time of the Roman occupation of Judea, the Emperor was moved to study Torah. He called the ten greatest rabbis to come to Rome and instruct him. Rabbi Ishmael was among them.

They began their study with the book of Genesis and all went well until they arrived at the passage in Exodus that says, "He who kidnaps a man, whether he sold him or is still holding him, shall be put to death" (Exodus 21:16). Suddenly the Emperor stopped reading and said, "Did we not read in Genesis that Joseph's ten brothers kidnapped him and sold him into slavery? Yet they were not killed. Does the law not apply to them?"

The sages assured the Emperor that it did, but that since the brothers had been dead for centuries there was no way to carry out the sentence. Outraged, the Emperor exclaimed, "You ten sages of Israel shall represent the ten brothers, and you shall die for their sin!"

The sages were arrested and placed together in a cell to await their deaths. The other sages turned to Rabbi Ishmael and begged him to use his mystic connection with God to overturn the Emperor's decree. Rabbi Ishmael assured them that he could do this, but that he would not do so unless he was certain that the Emperor was not in fact acting at the behest of God.

To find out the true source of the decree, Rabbi Ishmael put on his *tallit* and *tefillin* (prayer shawl and phylacteries) and began to intone a long prayer. As he prayed he ascended to heaven where he met the angel Gabriel who told him that the Emperor's decree was actually from God.

"By your deaths," Gabriel told him, "the evil that entered the world through the kidnapping of Joseph would be ended, and one of the chains that held back the Messiah from coming to earth would be broken." Their deaths, Gabriel said, would hasten the coming of Redemption, and they themselves would all be taken up and reunited in heaven.

Rabbi Ishmael returned to his cell and reported what he had learned to his friends. When they learned that their deaths had meaning, and that they would be reunited in heaven, each accepted his fate and went bravely to his death.[14]

For us the importance of this tale lies in Rabbi Ishmael's returning to earth after his ascent to heaven, in order to tell his comrades why their deaths are necessary and meaningful. The ascended ones are not content to escape this world, but return to it time and again to help those still bound to it.

The Ascension of Mary

Perhaps the most famous account of an ascended one is the ascension of Jesus. While often confused with Jesus's resurrection and the empty tomb, the ascension of Jesus actually takes place forty days after his resurrection.

The New Testament tells us of Jesus's ascension in the Gospel of Luke (Luke 24:50–53) and in the Acts of the Apostles (which also claims to be written by Luke). In the first chapter of Acts the resurrected Jesus responds to the apostles' question about the restoration of the kingdom of Israel by telling them that "it is not for you to know," and that God will do what is to be done in its proper time (Acts 1:7). Then, according to Acts, "When he had said this, as they were watching, he was lifted up, and a cloud took him out of their sight. While he was going and they were gazing up toward heaven, suddenly two men in white robes stood by them. They said, 'Men of Galilee, why do you stand looking up toward heaven? This Jesus, who has been taken up from you into heaven, will come in the same way as you saw him go into heaven'" (Acts 1:9–11).

The ascension of Jesus is a central part of Christian teaching attested to in both the Apostles' Creed and the Nicene Creed. And for countless Christians the ascension of Jesus and the ascension (assumption) of his mother, Mary, are not myths but historic occurrences.

But here we want to focus on the story itself, and on the question coming from the two men in white robes—angels to be sure—who ask the apostles why they are staring up into the sky.

On the surface the answer is, where else would they be staring? Jesus has just been lifted bodily into heaven with no warning or explanation. Who wouldn't stare? The fact that the angels pose the question suggests, however, that staring into the sky is not what the apostles *should* be doing. Borrowing from the insight of the Merkavah mystics who understood that the seeming ascent to the Throne of God is in fact a descent into the depths of the human, the angels may well be saying, "Yes, it seems that Jesus ascended, but if you wish to find him you must look *within*."

In Catholic doctrine the taking of Mary into heaven is called the assumption, and a distinction is made between ascension and assumption. For Catholics ascension means to ascend to heaven under one's own power. According to Christian doctrine, and despite the passive descriptions that Jesus "was taken up into heaven" (Mark 16:19), "was carried up into heaven" (Luke 24:51), and "he was lifted up" (Acts 1:9)—all suggesting that God lifted Jesus into heaven—this is what Jesus, as the second person of the Trinity, could and did do. His mother, not being a member of the Trinity, had no such power, and indeed had to be lifted up to heaven. This is the assumption. For our purposes, however, the distinction is not really relevant.

The actual place and time of Mary's death is unclear. Some say she lived for fifteen years following the death of her son, others say for only three. Some claim she died in Ephesus, and others believe it was in Jerusalem. According to one tradition, the archangel Michael appeared to Mary to tell her of her death. She pleaded with the angel to let her meet with the apostles one more time, and Michael magically transported them to her side at her deathbed. Jesus, too, came to be with his mother at her death, and when she died he took her soul to heaven. Three days later, Jesus returned and gathered up the body of Mary and took it to heaven as well where it was reunited with its soul under the Tree of Life in the Garden of Eden.

Focus on the death and assumption of Mary began during the restoration of Jerusalem as a Christian holy city under the reign of the Roman emperor Constantine (ca. 285–337). The city was leveled in 135 CE after the final Jewish revolt against Rome, and was rebuilt as *Aelia Capitolina* in honor of the Roman God Jupiter. Constantine's openness to Christianity as a way of unifying his fractious empire led to his mother's pilgrimage to Jerusalem and her naming, via revelation, of numerous holy sites. One of these was what was believed to be the Tomb of Mary, located close to Mount Zion.

On the mount itself was the place where, according to tradition, Mary fell asleep (died) before going to heaven. This so-called Place of Dormition was the site of an early Christian community, and is today the location of the Benedictine Abbey of the Dormition of Mary.

As bishops from throughout the Mediterranean world prepared to gather in Constantinople for the Council of Chalcedon in 451,

Emperor Marcian asked the patriarch of Jerusalem to bring with him relics of Mary that they may be enshrined in Constantinople. The patriarch explained to the emperor that there were no relics of Mary: while she had died in the presence of the apostles and was buried in a tomb, when that tomb was opened it was found empty. The apostles had concluded that Mary had risen bodily to heaven.

Feasts commemorating the death of Mary can be traced back to the fourth century, and St. Gregory of Tours (d. 594) set forth what may be the earliest formulation of the doctrine of Mary's being taken up into heaven. But despite the antiquity of the belief in the assumption of Mary, it did not become an official doctrine of the Catholic Church until November 1, 1950, when Pope Pius XII formally proclaimed: "Hence the revered Mother of God . . . like her own Son, having overcome death, she might be taken up body and soul to the glory of heaven where, as Queen, she sits in splendor at the right hand of her Son, the immortal King of the Ages . . . [B]y the authority of our Lord Jesus Christ, of the blessed Apostles Peter and Paul, and by Our own authority, We pronounce, declare, and define it to be a divinely revealed dogma: that the Immaculate Mother of God, the ever Virgin Mary, having completed the course of her earthly life, was assumed body and soul into heavenly glory . . ."[15]

The implication of the bodily assumption of Mary into heaven is a strong affirmation that not only the immaterial soul, but also the material body is suffused with spirit. As the scholar of Catholicism Peter Stravinskas explains,

> First of all, by Mary's Assumption, God reveals to us that His heavenly graces are meant to permeate every facet of our earthly, creaturely existence—even our very

bodies, our flesh and blood, with all their defects, deformities, disfigurements, and imperfections. At times we labor under a false assumption, namely, that God is not interested in our "bodiliness," but rather, only in our souls, the spiritual dimension in our existence.

However, the way God loves Mary, as she is bodily present to Him in heaven, is the way He loves us in our personal relationships with Him here on earth. In Mary's Assumption, God proves that His infinite love is neither selective nor exclusive, but that he loves us in the fullness of the integrity He has given us in creating His children as bodily human creatures.[16]

This understanding of the assumption of Mary speaks directly to our premise that the complete human being is capable of realizing the fullness of God, and is in fact born for that purpose. The descent of angels into the human realm, and the ascent of humans into the angelic realm, are symbolic representations of this capacity. According to Peter Stravinskas,

> In calling Mary to Himself, body and soul, in the Assumption, God reconfirms that His love perfects not only our immaterial souls but also our very material, physical bodies. In loving us this way, and in demonstrating that love through the Assumption of Mary, God teaches us anew how we are to love ourselves, and the sanctified way in which we are to regard our lives. For just as God transported and elevated the body and soul of His Mother, so too will He transport and elevate every dimension of our human

lives *now* [author's emphasis] as we remain united with Him in Mary . . .'[17]

In our daily lives, we know daily deaths as, over and over again, we are called to die to self and live for God. Many times the false assumption beleaguers us that, if we are suffering, it is because we have done something wrong, or because God no longer cares for us.[18]

These "daily deaths," the spiritual death of the self that our ego-centered mind imagines us to be, is in fact the birth of our angelic potential and its ability to lift us heavenward—not lifted bodily to another place, but awakened bodily to the divine fullness of the here and now.

Appearances of the Virgin Mary are examples of the God-centered spirit embodied in a fully realized human. Mary represents the human capacity to move through ego-centered mind to world-centered soul and God-centered spirit, and then to return to the domain of the ego-centered minds to point those minds toward the greater reality of which they are a part.

According to Catholic tradition the first appearance of Mary on earth after her ascent to heaven occurred around the year 40 when James, the brother of John, was traveling in Saragossa (Zaragoza), Spain. Depressed over the way his mission was progressing, James was preaching on the banks of the Ebro River when Mary and an angelic host appeared to him. She gave him a statue of herself and a six-foot wooden pillar on which to place it. She said to him, "This place is to be my house, and this image and column shall be the title and altar of the temple you shall build." Reinvigorated by Mary's visit, James set about to build a small chapel in her honor.[19] Today, while the site itself has been demolished and rebuilt numerous times, the statue and pillar are still honored at the Basilica-Cathedral of Our Lady of the Pillar in Zaragoza.

One of the most famous appearances of Mary was in Guadalupe, Mexico, in 1531. Throughout the previous decades the Spanish conquistadors had battled with the indigenous Aztecs, leading to fierce abuses by the European invaders. Outraged, the Aztec leaders threatened to slaughter every Spaniard in the country, including the many missionaries seeking to bring the Aztecs into the Church. A fifty-seven-year-old peasant named Juan Diego was one of the natives who had converted to Catholicism.

> Walking to mass one day, Juan Diego heard birds singing from a nearby hilltop. As he drew near the summit of the hill to investigate, the chirping ceased, and Juan Diego heard the voice of a woman calling him, "Juan, Juan Diego, Juanito." Upon reaching the summit, he saw a stunning Aztec girl around the age of fourteen. Speaking to him in his own tongue, she told Juan Diego that she was the Virgin Mary, and that a church was to be built for her on this hilltop. She asked Juan to go to Mexico City and tell the bishop of her request.
>
> Juan did as he was asked, but the bishop refused to take him seriously. Juan returned to the Virgin and was told by her to try a second time. When he reapproached the bishop, he was asked to produce a sign that this was indeed a request from the Virgin Mary.
>
> Juan again returned to the hilltop and told Mary of the bishop's requirement. Mary told Juan to return to her the next morning at dawn. When Juan returned to

his home, however, he found his uncle very ill. He nursed his uncle all night and through the following day, missing his dawn meeting with the Virgin.

Certain his uncle was dying, Juan rushed into town to find a priest. As he passed the hill where the Virgin had spoken with him, Mary again appeared to him. He explained his predicament, and she promised him that his uncle was getting better even as they spoke. She said to Juan, "Hear me, my littlest son: Let nothing discourage you, nothing depress you. Let nothing alter your heart or your countenance. Do not fear any illness, anxiety, or pain. Am I not your mother? Are you not under the protection of my mantle? Am I not your fountain of life? Is there anything else that you need?"

She then asked Juan to climb the hill and pick flowers and take them to the bishop as the sign he had requested. This was the coldest month of the year when flowers did not grow, yet when Juan reached the hilltop it was covered with Castilian roses. Juan returned to Mary and showed her the roses. She took them and wove them into his *tilma*, a cloak worn by the Aztecs and traditionally made of cactus fibers. She told Juan to take the tilma to the bishop and let no one handle it but the bishop.

So Juan Diego went once more to Mexico City and met with the bishop. Refusing to let anyone take his cloak, he waited until the bishop would see him. He then opened the tilma. The roses fell to the floor, and in their place on the tilma was the glowing image of Mary as the young Aztec woman that Juan Diego had met.

Now convinced that this was indeed the Virgin Mary, the bishop accompanied Juan to the hilltop. Later the bishop's assistants went with Juan to see his uncle who by this time had fully recovered, and who himself had met with the Virgin Mary. She had told him that the image on Juan's tilma was to be called Santa Maria de Guadalupe.

The key to this story is Mary's words to Juan Diego, "Am I not your mother? Are you not under the protection of my mantle? Am I not your fountain of life?" Mary is the Mother of God, and yet here she says she is also the Mother of Juan Diego. Jesus says, "I am the way, and the truth, and the life. No one comes to the Father except through me" (John 14:6), yet here Mary is the fountain of life, the source of life, that out of which life comes as Jesus came out of his mother.

Mary heals, Mary succors, Mary provides in the same way that God the Son and God the Father do. What this means is that the ascending and descending Virgin, like the angels and other ascended humans who rise to heaven and return to earth as messengers of the divine, are not signs of God, but manifestations of God. They do not point to something other than themselves; they are themselves that very Spirit—and so are we.

The message of the ascended humans is that we, too, have this potential. We, too, can realize ourselves as the Divine. We are the image of God, and we can realize our own divinity and embrace the world in a godly manner.

Over the centuries there have been dozens and dozens of appearances of the Virgin Mary; here are some of the major ones:

Sometime around the year 1061 Mary appeared to the widow Lady Richeldis de Faverches who lived in Walsingham, England. Lady Richeldis had three visions of Mary, and in each one she was shown the house in Nazareth where the angel Gabriel had announced to Mary that she was to give birth to Jesus. Mary asked that a replica of this house be built that "all who are in any way distressed or in need seek me there in that small house that you maintain for me at Walsingham. To all that seek me there shall be given succor."

The house was built and became a place of pilgrimage for kings and commoners throughout Europe. Eventually a church was built over the house to protect it from wear. Both church and house were destroyed in the 1530s when King Henry VIII broke with the Catholic Church, established the Church of England, and ordered the destruction of Catholic monasteries and shrines in the country.

What was the purpose of reconstructing the house of the annunciation? It was to be a place for meeting Mary and finding comfort. Metaphorically speaking, the house Lady Richeldis de Faverches saw in her visions was not a physical structure but the inner house, the angelic faculty within each of us.

Mary appeared in La Vang, Vietnam, at the end of the eighteenth century. For much of the century the country had been in turmoil, because of warlords from the north and south and peasant revolts. Three brothers from Tay Son led a revolt that defeated warlords on both sides and united the country under a single king. One of the southern warlords, Nguyen Anh, sought refuge with the French Catholic mission on Phu Quoc Island, and the bishop convinced him to seek a military alliance with King Louis XVI.

King Canh Thinh, worried that the Catholic connections of Nguyen Anh would turn the Catholics in his united Vietnam against him, sought to suppress Catholicism. Nguyen Anh did defeat Canh Thinh, but did not end the anti-Catholic tyranny. Indeed, he intensified it. It was during this time of persecution that Mary appeared to the people of Vietnam. She was called the Lady of La Vang, perhaps for the forest of La Vang trees in which she first appeared in 1798, though the name could also be derived from the Vietnamese word for "crying out." Mary continued to appear to the Vietnamese in the forest for one hundred years, each time offering comfort and solace for a people whose lives were mired in tragedy.

The appearance of Mary to the fourteen-year-old Bernadette Soubirous in Lourdes, France, in 1858 is well known. Bernadette did not fathom Mary's identity until the last of the eighteen visits from Mary, when she revealed herself to the girl saying, "I am the Immaculate Conception." Mary urged that a hole be dug in a grotto in order for a spring to appear, whose waters would bring healing to those who sought it. The Church declared the apparitions authentic in 1862, and millions of pilgrims ever since have found comfort there. Tragically, Bernadette, who had joined the sisters of Notre Dame in Nevers, died in 1879 after a protracted and painful illness.

Digging inside a grotto, going deep within to release the healing waters contained there, again speaks to our understanding that these visions are ultimately leading us to an inner discovery, the ending of the illusion of *achad*, and the transformation toward wholeness.

Appearances of St. Francis of Assisi
Mary is not the only Catholic saint to return to earth after her death. St. Francis of Assisi (ca. 1181–1226) is also said to have periodically returned to earth as a teacher and guide. Perhaps the most famous account of this is found in the book *The Little Flowers of St. Francis of*

Assisi. These brief chapters on the life of St. Francis were probably composed around 1275. Officially the author of *The Little Flowers* remains anonymous, but scholars believe that the book was written by Ugolino di Monte Santa Maria, whose name appears three times in the earliest manuscript of *The Little Flowers*.

It is in the chapter entitled "How St. Francis Appeared, After His Death, To Brother John of Alvernia, While He Was In Prayer" that we find this example of a fully realized human being returning from heaven to speak to other humans:

> St Francis once appeared on Mount Alvernia to Brother John of Alvernia, a man of great sanctity, while he was in prayer, and spoke with him for a long space of time; and before he departed he said to him: "Ask of me what thou wilt." Then Brother John made answer: "Father, I pray thee, tell me that which I have long desired to know,— what thou wast doing, and where thou wast, when the seraph appeared to thee." And St Francis replied: "I was praying in that place whereon the chapel of Count Simon da Battifolle now stands, and I asked two favours of my Lord Jesus Christ. The first was that he would grant to me in my lifetime to feel, as far as might be possible, both in my soul and body, all that he had suffered in his most bitter Passion. The second favour which I asked was, that I might feel in my heart that exceeding love which enkindled his, and moved him to endure so great a Passion for us sinners. And then God put it into my heart that it was granted to me to feel both, as far as is possible for a mere creature; and this promise was well

fulfilled to me by the impression of the stigmata." Then
Brother John asked him whether those sacred words
spoken to him by the seraph had been truly related by
the brother who affirmed that he had heard them from
the mouth of St Francis, in the presence of eight friars.
And St Francis made answer, that they were even so as
that brother had said.[20]

While we have no record of what St. Francis told Brother John
during the initial hours of his visit, their closing conversation is
clear enough. Brother John has questions regarding St. Francis's
own mystical experiences. He doesn't ask his questions to overcome doubts as to the authenticity of St. Francis as a great saint
and mystic, but to somehow participate in the experience Francis
himself had.

Brother John inquires as to the authenticity of the legends regarding St. Francis and the seraph, and Francis confirms that they are
true. More importantly, however, Brother John wants to know what
it was Francis was doing when the seraph appeared to him.

The appearance of a seraph, the highest order of angels in
medieval Christianity, perhaps even equivalent to Metatron, the
Lesser YHVH of Jewish mythology, is revealing. A seraph is closest
to God and dwells in the highest of heavenly realms. For St. Francis
to encounter a seraph he himself must have ascended into those
realms. This is reminiscent of the vision of Isaiah in which he
ascends from Solomon's Temple in Jerusalem to the heavenly court
of God surrounded by flaming, six-winged seraphim (Isaiah 6:1–13).
St. Francis is said to have had his encounter with the seraph while
praying on Mount La Verna in Tuscany.

In addition to meeting the seraph St. Francis saw the crucified Christ and received from him the stigmata, physical piercings of St. Francis's own hands, feet, and side as signs of his personal transformation into a Christ-like being. In other words, Francis's encounter with the seraph marks the transformation from ego-centered mind and world-centered soul to fully God-centered spirit. Through suffering the ego-centered mind opens to the world-centered soul and begins to feel the pain of the world. The next stage is to translate this suffering into love, much as a parent feels the pain of a child and finds in that shared suffering a deeper love for that child and the world.

Brother John then asks in effect how he, too, may undergo such a transformation. St. Francis reveals to John that he was indeed praying for just that. He wanted to experience and embody the suffering of Christ that he might thereby manifest Christly love for the world.

Brother John now shifts from the historical to the immediate: could he see and touch and kiss the saint's stigmata and thereby experience in a lesser way what Francis had experienced in the presence of the seraph? Perhaps John knows that he does not have the imaginative or spiritual power to meet a seraph himself, but that by touching one who did, he might partake of that experience as well.

Clearly, this is the role of the human who has risen to the heavens and returns to earth: to provide a doorway through which we others might also move from ego-centered mind through world-centered soul to God-centered spirit. Lastly St. Francis invites Brother John to touch the nail piercing his palm, and as he does so a cloud of incense is released. The fragrance enters John's nostrils just as God breathes the breath of life into the nostrils of *adam* (humanity) in Genesis 2:7. In Genesis *adam* becomes conscious; in *The Little Flowers* Brother John becomes fully conscious, "rapt in God," and lost in a state of ecstasy for a full hour. This is the state of I-I, when the ego is totally absorbed into the divine so that no sense of *achad*, separateness, remains.

The Ascension of Muhammad

The most famous story of ascension in Islam is the Night Journey of Muhammad from Mecca to Jerusalem to heaven. We are introduced to the notion of the Night Journey in the Qur'an: "Glory to Him who took His votary to a wide and open land from the Sacred Mosque (at Makkah) to the distant Mosque whose precincts We have blessed, that We may show him some of Our signs. Verily He is all-hearing and all-seeing" (Qur'an 17:1).[21]

This sliver of a story is expanded in the Hadith. The journey itself took place a few years after the beginning of Muhammad's prophetic mission. While the Prophet was steadfast in his faith in Allah and the task Allah had set for him, others were not so sure, and Muhammad was feeling alone and isolated.

One midsummer night Muhammad slept in a house near the Kaaba in Mecca. While he slept the archangel Jibril (Gabriel) entered his room and washed Muhammad's chest with water from the sacred well of *Zamzam* in Mecca, and in this way removed all doubt from the Prophet.

With a golden beaker Gabriel then poured over Muhammad wisdom, *hikma* (*Chochma* in Hebrew, *Sophia* in Greek). The angel then took the Prophet's hand and led him to the winged horse Buraq. Riding Buraq, Muhammad flew from Mecca to Mount Sinai, from Sinai to the tomb of Abraham in Hebron, from Hebron to Bethlehem and the birthplace of Jesus, and finally from Bethlehem to Jerusalem. After tethering Buraq, Muhammad is met by Abraham, Moses, and Jesus whom he leads in prayer. As a sign of his having been in Jerusalem, Muhammad leaves his footprint on the rock that is today the centerpiece of the Dome of the Rock, the third most holy site in Islam.

The second part of Muhammad's journey, the ascension, begins with the conclusion of these prayers. Muhammad and Gabriel then ascend through the different levels of heaven. At each of the seven levels of heaven Muhammad encounters angels of various kinds, including one who appears as a White Cock and whose feet rest on earth while his head grazes the Throne of God, another who is made half of fire and half of snow, and a number of angels with seventy heads or faces. The angels seem to represent the enormousness of the places through which Muhammad travels, and may simply be symbolic of that.

As Muhammad reaches each level of heaven he is confronted by a door guarded by an angel whose task it is to prevent unlawful entry. The archangel Gabriel knocks at each door, and the "dwellers of the Heaven ask, 'Who is it?' He replies, 'Gabriel.' They respond, 'Who is accompanying you?' Gabriel says, 'Muhammad.' They say, 'Has he been called?' Gabriel tells them, 'Yes,' and the Dwellers of the Heaven reply, 'He is welcome.'"[22]

It is important to note that only the called are welcome. What does it mean to be called? In the story of Isaiah, the one who is called is the one who answers God's need for a messenger. Isaiah says, "Here! Send me!" (Isaiah 6:8). When we are willing and able to say "Here! Send me!" to God, we show that we are willing and able to step out of our ego-centered consciousness and surrender to the will of God— "not what I want but what you want" (Matthew 26:39). Then we are welcome to the process of ascension and transformation.

At last the Prophet reaches the *Sidrat el-Muntaha*, the "lotus of extremity," where he sees a tree sprouting emerald and pearl branches growing on the right side of God's Throne. At the base of the tree are the source waters of the Nile, the Euphrates, and two other rivers of Paradise, the Selsebil and the Kawthar, whose water is said to be whiter than milk and sweeter than honey.

Three unnamed angels then approach the Prophet, each offering him a cup of refreshment: one carrying milk, the second carrying wine, and the third offering honey. Muhammad chooses only the milk, and the angels praise him for his wisdom.

Wine is the way of intoxication. Taken to the extreme wine is a path to selflessness but not transformation: a drunk may lose his inhibitions and even his sense of self, but nothing positive comes from this loss.

Honey is the way of pleasure, sweetness. While this may be part of the divine journey of transformation, if we are not also willing to descend into the shadow realms and bring about a transformation of the dark side of life, our transformation is incomplete.

Milk gives life. Unlike wine or honey, it has the power to sustain new life and nourish it. Yet if it is not drunk when offered, if it is allowed to sit unused, it sours. If Muhammad had not chosen the milk, it would have gone bad, suggesting that the gift of God must be grasped when offered: one who hesitates is lost.

The archangel Gabriel then addresses Muhammad, saying, "I can accompany you no further," and instructing the Prophet to approach the *Sidrat el-Muntaha* alone. Muhammad complies with Gabriel's request, and leaves the angel behind. When he draws near to the Throne of God he prostrates himself in front of it. As his head touches the ground the angels cry out, "We bear witness that the Most-High is the One and Living, and that there is no other god but Him, and that Muhammad is His servant and messenger."[23]

As with the angels who reach out to help humanity, so the Prophet rises to heaven only to return to earth to serve humanity. Isaiah ascends to God and returns as God's messenger. Mary ascends and returns time and again to show other humans their angelic potential. And Muhammad ascends and returns with the Way of *Salat*, the Way of Prayer that is the second of the five pillars of Islam. In other words, the point of the journey is to transform the journeyer so that he or she can teach others how to transform themselves.

The Ascension of Dhruv

Ascension narratives exist in Eastern traditions as well as in the West. One of the most famous of these in Hinduism is the story of Dhruv in the *Bhagavata Purana*, the "Book of God," which scholars date to the ninth or tenth century CE, but which Hindu tradition believes was composed about 3100 BCE.

In the *Bhagavata Purana* we learn of five-year-old Dhruv who asked his father to lift him up and put him on his father's lap, next to his half-brother Uttam. Uttam's mother Suruchi—reminiscent of Sarah in the story of Hagar, Ishmael, and Isaac—was outraged that the son of her husband's second wife, Suneeti, would dare to claim equality with her son Uttam. Suruchi berated the boy and Dhruv ran home to seek comfort from his mother.

> Suneeti explained to Dhruv that he would always be disappointed when asking things from humans, and that he should reserve his requests for God alone. She told him that Suruchi had done him a favor in showing him the shallowness of human generosity, and

demanded that Dhruv go into the forest, do penance, and pray for the welfare of Suruchi.

"I am not sending you to the forest alone," Suneeti said to Dhruv, "for my blessings and God are with you."

As soon as Dhruv entered the forest he met Naradji, one of the immortal sages, who, after urging the boy to be a boy and play, instructed Dhruv how to pray the mantrum, *Om Namo Bhagavate Vasudevaya,* "I offer my respects to the Great Lord." Dhruv went home and for the next six months spent an ever-longer amount of time in meditation using the mantrum taught to him by Naradji.

Impressed by Dhruv's devotion, God appeared to him. The boy's eyes were closed, however, and he was focused on an image of God that had appeared in his own heart. God took on that form, and caused the image in Dhruv's heart to fade. Dhruv opened his eyes and saw God standing in front of him. Dhruv exclaimed, "You are the one who is also within me! You are the one that makes my senses come alive! You are the one who kindles my intellect!"

God asked what it was that he might bestow on Dhruv, and the boy said that his only desire was to receive whatever the Lord wished to give. Knowing that Dhruv had only wanted to sit on his father's lap, God took the boy with him into heaven and sat Dhruv on his lap. From then until now we can look into the heavens and see Dhruv sitting on the divine father's lap, looking to all below as the North Star.

The myth of Dhruv seems to lack the return to humankind that other ascension stories contain, but once we look a bit closer we realize that Dhruv is a boon to humanity. The key lies in his becoming the North Star.

The North Star has been used for navigation for millennia, both to locate the direction of north and to determine one's latitude. Becoming the North Star is the way the myth tells us that Dhruv becomes our guiding star. He points to the awareness of God as the True North, the inner spiritual direction by which we can navigate our lives from ego-centered mind through world-centered soul to God-centered spirit. When we peer into the night sky and see the North Star, Dhruv reminds us of the true nature of God as the one who is within as well as without.

The Ascension of Dharmakara

One of the best-known examples of ascension in Buddhism differs from those we have encountered so far in the same way that Buddhism itself differs from other religions. The Buddha was persistently silent about most things metaphysical, yet as Buddhism entered China in the first century CE, it began to incorporate indigenous Chinese ideas and develop new forms of devotion. While Pure Land Buddhism had its origins in India, it began to flourish in East Asia after the Pure Land Sutras were translated from Sanskrit into Chinese in 148 CE. The Pure Land was at first thought to be a place one could go to after death and from which one could attain enlightenment. Over time the Pure Land came to stand for enlightenment itself, and was thought to be a state of mind attainable here and now. Both ideas coexist in modern Pure Land communities.

In our context the most important of the Pure Land sutras is the *Sutra of Immeasurable Life*, in which the historic Buddha, Siddhartha Gotama, tells the story of Dharmakara (Storehouse of the Dharma/Teaching) who became Amida Buddha, the Buddha of Infinite Light.

Dharmakara, the hero of the sutra, was an Indian king who lived in the prehistoric time of Lokesvaraja Buddha, one of the innumerable mythic predecessors of the historic Buddha, Siddhartha Gotama. Dharmakara heard the *dharma* (teaching) of Lokesvaraja Buddha, and immediately surrendered his throne to devote himself to it. His aim was to become a Buddha and create a *buddhaksetra*, a Buddha-field or perfect heavenly abode from which others could achieve enlightenment. This *buddhakestra* was called the Pure Land.

In the process of becoming a disciple of Lokesvaraja, Dharmakara took upon himself forty-eight vows, promising that unless and until all forty-eight were fulfilled he would refrain from entering Nirvana and attaining enlightenment. Central among the forty-eight vows was the eighteenth vow, called the Primal Vow: "If I were to become a Buddha, and people, hearing my Name, have faith and joy and recite it for even ten times, but were not born in my Pure Land, may I not gain enlightenment."[24]

In other words, Dharmakara forsook his own enlightenment until he could effect the enlightenment of all others. And Dharmakara's nineteenth vow promised that he would appear to all those who called upon him at the moment of their death, regardless of their level of spiritual or moral attainment.

Dharmakara devoted himself to his practice and awoke from the I-It of ego-centered mind to the I-I of God-centered spirit (to use our terms). Here is what Dharmakara as Amida Buddha attained:

No thought of greed, anger, or harmfulness arose in his mind; he cherished no impulse of greed, anger, or harmfulness. He did not cling to objects or perception—color, sound, smell, taste. Abounding in perseverance, he gave no thought to the suffering to be endured. He was content with few desires, and without greed, anger, or folly. Always tranquil in a state of *samadhi* (concentration), he possessed wisdom that knew no impediment. He was free of all thoughts of falsity or deception. Gentle in countenance and loving in speech, he perceived people's thoughts and was attentive to them. He was full of courage and vigor, and being resolute in his acts, knew no fatigue. Seeking solely that which was pure and undefiled, he brought benefit to all beings.[25]

This notion of the Pure Land first appeared in the Chinese Buddhist tradition as *ching-t'u* (*Jodo* in Japanese). At first *ching-t'u* was thought to be the ideal place for spiritual realization. The Pure Land, not unlike heaven in Western religious thought, was somewhere outside the distractions of the world where one could focus solely on achieving the highest spiritual goals.

Over the centuries Pure Land Buddhism came from China to Japan, and in the tenth century CE a Japanese monk named Genshin established an elite religious society whose members sought to visualize the Pure Land, and in this way attain rebirth there after death. Again, Genshin's understanding of the Pure Land is comparable to the Christian notion of heaven: a paradise replete with singing birds, bell-covered trees, and celestial music, and a place in which one is reunited with loved ones.

To help laypeople attain the Pure Land after death, it became popular among Japanese Buddhists to place a screen adorned with the painted figure of Amida Buddha peering down from mountain peaks at the head of the bed of a dying person. A string was tied connecting the hand of the dying person to Amida Buddha so that at death the Buddha of Infinite Light would haul the soul into the Pure Land where it would engage in long and vigorous spiritual training that would eventually lead the soul to Nirvana.

This earlier notion of the Pure Land as a place of practice to be reached after death and ultimately to be transcended began to shift in the twelfth century. No longer was Amida Buddha limited to a heavenly abode after life: he was now depicted as speaking to the living, inviting them to join him in this life—in a way not unlike other descended ones who return to earth to help humans to transform themselves.

Shinran (1173–ca. 1263), a Japanese Buddhist monk and student of Honen (who had established a major Pure Land tradition in Japan in the late twelfth century), radically redefined the notion of Pure Land. For Shinran rebirth in the Pure Land did not refer to an after-death incarnation in a heavenly realm. Rather, "rebirth in the Pure Land" for him was synonymous with enlightenment. It happens in this life, in the midst of one's ordinary affairs. If we surrender ourselves completely to Amida Buddha, who represents pure I-I awareness, we are "immediately . . . without any passage of time, without any passage of days"[26] reborn in the Pure Land.

For Shinran the Pure Land was no longer an otherworldly place but a state of realization in the here and now. "Unlike the traditional view that required a long period of training in the Pure Land before attaining Buddhahood, Shinran affirmed supreme enlightenment at the moment of death by virtue of the working of great compassion. Furthermore, since perfect enlightenment is attained in the Pure Land, one returns immediately to *samsara* (the ordinary world) for the salvation of all beings. Thus the Pure Land is not the final destination; it is a way station on the return trip to *samsara* . . . The ultimate goal of a Shin Buddhist is not personal salvation but the deliverance of all beings from *samsara*."[27]

This reinvention of the Pure Land as a state of enlightenment so filled with compassion that all who attain it return to the ego-centered realm to help others do the same is the full realization of the meaning of the ascension myths. Here it is not enough that exceptional spiritual individuals are taken to heaven and return to earth to be messengers of God. In Shinran's vision *all* of us, regardless of our level of spiritual attainment, and due simply to the overwhelming love of Amida Buddha, will ascend to the Pure Land, realize the greater unity of God, woman, man, and nature, and return to the world of ordinary ego-centered consciousness to share this truth with others.

Eight

Lectio Divina
and the Angelic Way

ﻌﻌﻌ

AT THE HEART of this book is the intuition that we are part of God, and the notion that myths regarding angels are designed to remind us of that. The stories of angels descending to earth and taking on human form, the stories of humans ascending to heaven and becoming angels, the stories of humans ascending to heaven to see God, and the stories of humans ascending to heaven and then returning to earth to guide humanity are all pointing to a single truth: humanity and God belong to a singular reality, and each has the capacity to reach the other.

In other words, the relationship between humanity and God is analogous to that between the positive and negative poles of a magnet. A magnet cannot be a magnet without both poles, and neither pole can exist without its opposite. Yet it is the nature of the human mind, trapped as it is in the illusion of *achad*, the alienation from the whole, to imagine itself separate from God. This imagined division is the cause of much suffering on our part: feeling alienated from the whole we seek to become whole in and of ourselves, like a wave pretending to be the ocean or a leaf pretending to be the tree. While we can easily see the absurdity of this when speaking of waves and leaves, it is much more difficult for us to see the absurdity of the very same kind of thinking when it comes to ourselves.

And yet we cannot shake off our deep sense that the state of *achad* is not real, that there is more to us than our ego-centered mind lets on. The ego-centered mind cannot shut off or dismiss the insights of the world-centered soul and God-centered spirit. These larger Wholes, Wholes that embrace the ego in a greater nondual reality, continually break into our ego-centered world, and one way in which they do so is as angels.

Thus we understand angels as metaphors for the human capacity to both transcend and include ego-centered mind in more holistic levels of consciousness that ultimately realize the divinity that is the fully human. We are to realize our true nature as part of God, the singularity that is all reality.

The Greeks called this process of divinization *apotheosis* (from Greek "to deify"). According to Joseph Campbell apotheosis is one of the stages of the Hero's Journey—the monomyth that underlies almost all mythic tales across times and cultures. Campbell described seventeen steps or states in this monomyth, and while most myths do not contain all seventeen, the three major divisions into which the seventeen stages fall do seem to be universal. They are "Departure," "Initiation," and "Return."

Departure calls the hero to a quest which takes him or her away from the known; Initiation happens when the hero passes a number of tests or trials and is rewarded with some new insight or level of self-awareness that has practical application; and Return refers to the conclusion of the myth when the hero returns to the ordinary world and uses the new insight or skill to improve the world. Apotheosis occurs during the Initiation stage where the hero's very idea of reality is changed, and he or she can now engage the world in a new way. The apotheosis often entails an expansion of consciousness that shatters the more narrow view of the ego-centered mind. Along with this new consciousness comes a sense of self-sacrifice: the hero is willing to sacrifice the self for the greater good.

As Joseph Campbell once said, "Myths do not belong, properly, to the rational mind. Rather, they bubble up from deep in the wells of what Carl Jung called the collective unconscious."[1] Or to use our own wording: myths do not belong, properly, to the ego-centered mind. Rather they break into that mind from the larger, more inclusive fields of consciousness we call world-centered soul and God-centered spirit. Our myths about angels reflect insights of which our ego-centered minds are largely unaware.

To speak of myth in this way we need to recall that while the word "myth" is today often and erroneously linked to the words "false" and "lie," the original and truer meaning of the word is still viable. "[M]ythology is not a lie, mythology is poetry, it is metaphorical. It has been well said that mythology is the penultimate truth—penultimate because the ultimate cannot be put into words. It is beyond words, beyond images . . . Mythology pitches the mind . . . to what can be known but not told. So this is the penultimate truth."[2]

The truth toward which the myths of angels point is the truth of the absolute unity of all reality in, with, and as God. Actively engaging with myths of angels tilts our thinking and opens our minds to more holistic ways of knowing and living in the world. In Campbell's words, "It's important to live life with the experience, and therefore the knowledge, of its mystery and your own mystery. This gives life a new radiance, a new harmony, a new splendor. Thinking in mythological terms helps to put you in accord with the inevitables of this vale of tears. You learn to recognize the positive values in what appear to be the negative moments and aspects of your life. The big question is whether you are going to be able to say a hearty yes to your adventure . . . the adventure of the hero—the adventure of being alive."[3]

Angels, or more accurately our myths of angels, call us to the adventure of life, the hero's journey from bounded ego-centered consciousness to unbounded divine consciousness. Angels are our mythic guides to this greater reality. They point toward a truth greater than themselves and show us how to realize that truth in and as our truest selves. In some of the myths the hero becomes the angel and returns to guide us to the place he or she has been to. In others the angel speaks to the hero as "other" and yet is internal—what Rabbi Joseph Karo (1488–1575), the great master of Jewish jurisprudence who said he was visited by an angel he called the Maggid (the Proclaimer), called an "echo" of our deepest thoughts.

According to Karo, the Maggid visited him regularly for fifty-two years. A journal of his encounters with the Maggid was published some time after Karo's death under the title *Maggid Mesharim* ("One

Who Proclaims What Is True"), a phrase borrowed from Isaiah: "I didn't whisper secrets in a land of shadow; I didn't say to Jacob's descendants, 'Look for me in bedlam.' I, YHVH, speak what is just, I proclaim what is true [*maggid mesharim*]" (Isaiah 45:19).

In his journal Karo wrote, "Said the Maggid to Karo: 'I am only the echo of your thoughts.'"[4] The Maggid reveals to Karo, and through his journal to us, the true nature of angels—echos of our own thoughts. Not the thoughts generated by the *achad*-plagued ego-centered mind, but thoughts liberated from illusion and reflective of the greater wholeness to which each of us belongs.

This understanding of angels as an echo of our own thoughts is key to the premise of this book. Angels are inner realities, inner capacities of human consciousness accessible to us when we transcend the ego-centered limits of self and attune to the larger truth of reality found in the divine realms.

Over the course of five decades the Maggid revealed many secrets to Joseph Karo, secrets that he dutifully recorded in his journal. "I came to reveal to you the mystery of mysteries, the secret of secrets," the Maggid tells Karo. "What I am going to tell you now will make the bones rattle and the knees tremble in fear, terror, and awe."[5] Why? Because they reveal dimensions of reality that the ego-centered mind cannot fathom, and may well fear.

All angels reveal secrets, even the fallen ones. Satan calls us to face our dark side, and does so with all the skill he can muster. Where would be the heroic in our journey if the dark side was portrayed as not alluring? It takes little courage to say "no" to the undesirable. So Satan makes the dark side seem appealing, and does his best to entice us to it. That is his task—to make our choosing between good and evil real and courageous.

The question is whether or not we are willing to say "yes" to the angels, "yes" to our own transformation, and "yes" to the hero's journey that might cost us all we know and yet promises us so much more.

Here, in *The Angelic Way*, we want to assume that we are willing to say "yes"—if not this moment, then the next; if not today, then perhaps tomorrow. And with this assumption we will explore how we can evoke our angelic potential and open us to the greater wholeness of which we are a part.

To evoke something is to call it into our consciousness from within. Angels do not dwell outside of us, but inside of us. They are, as Joseph Karo's angel revealed, echoes of our own higher mind, aspects of ourselves that our ego-centered mind cannot grasp due to its state of *achad*.

But to evoke the angelic we have to engage the ego. We cannot "slay the ego" and discover the angelic, for who would be doing the slaying? "We" *are* for the most part ego-centered minds, and there is no need to deny, decry, or defeat that truth. Like Karo we must engage in ego-centered activities that will draw out the angels rather than drown out the ego.

Joseph Karo's method was a type of *lectio divina*, a contemplative reading of the Mishnah, the early law code of the ancient rabbis—not as a fixed text to be memorized but as a fluid field in which to let the imagination play with possibility. At the heart of angelic encounters is this willingness to let the imagination play. By actively and imaginatively entering into the classic myths of angels we can evoke the angelic mind and receive our own revelation.

Lectio Divina

What we are suggesting is to use our imagination to engage our angelic faculty by reading and listening to the myths of angels, ascending humans, and human and angelic messengers in a specific way, a way rooted in the spiritual practice of *lectio divina*.

Lectio divina, Latin for "divine reading" or "holy reading," is a traditional Christian prayer practice nurtured in Benedictine monasteries and designed to act as a catalyst for communion with God. Lectio divina can be found in the monastic rules of Pachomius (ca. 292–348), Basil (ca. 330–379), Augustine (354–430), and Benedict (ca. 480-ca. 547), though the formal structuring of the practice into four steps or stages dates back to the Carthusian monk Guigo II in his book *The Monk's Ladder*, dating to around 1150.

While we will adapt lectio divina to our own needs, it may help to understand the process as it was originally articulated. Lectio divina is usually an hour-long discipline, though some people divide the practice into two half-hour periods, one in the morning, the other at night.

Lectio divina should be done in a peaceful setting. The reading one wishes to use should be chosen in advance. Prior to reading one should take a few minutes to quiet body and mind. Once feeling centered one should begin the four stages of lectio divina. The first stage is *lectio*, reading the chosen passage slowly and with full attention several times through. The second stage is *meditatio*, thinking over the meaning and implication of words or sentences. The third stage is *oratio*, entering into an inner dialogue with God around the passage just read. The fourth stage is *contemplatio*, a silent resting in the presence of God.

To pursue our angelic lectio divina, we first need to set aside a specific place and time to engage in spiritual reading. The place should be quiet and free from distractions, and the time should be one when we are least apt to be intruded upon either in person or electronically.

Second, we need to choose a myth about angels with which we wish to engage. There is nothing magical about this choice; one myth is not better than another. Rather, we should choose a passage that speaks to us personally. If we find ourselves drawn to the tales of the archangels, let us choose one of the passages relating to them. If Hindu or Buddhist myths move us, we can choose from among them. But there is no need to be interreligious in one's choice. While over time we may choose to draw from myths that are presently outside of our comfort zone or area of interest, we are most likely to have success with this spiritual reading if we choose a passage that we find intrinsically moving or intriguing. In a sense we should let the myth choose us, rather than our choosing the myth.

Third, as we begin to settle into our reading, we need to make time to quiet our body and mind. Our body should be comfortable, our breathing soft, even, and slow—but we don't want to fall asleep. We rest our attention on our breath, focus lightly on our inhalation and exhalation. We shouldn't seek to control our breathing, just watch it. Over time we will fall into a natural rhythm, and we will be ready to proceed.

Lectio

First we read the selected passage aloud slowly. Reading aloud slows the reading down and with it our breath. There is no rush. At first we may wish to exaggerate the reading a bit, pausing between clauses.

In the following example of a possible reading, the Prophet Elijah has fled from his enemies into the desert, and is full of despair. He lies down under a tree, deeply exhausted, and falls asleep. Twice an angel appears to him with food and water, and thus strengthened Elijah moves on and walks for many days until he reaches Mount

Horeb and settles in a cave there for the night. Then God speaks to Elijah:

> "Leave [the cave] and position yourself on the mountain before YHVH, Who is passing by." Suddenly a terrible wind tore through the mountains crushing boulders to pieces before YHVH, but YHVH was not in the wind; as the wind grew still the earth quaked, but YHVH was not in the earthquake; and following the earthquake a fire blazed, but YHVH was not in the fire; and after the fire cooled—a voice of fragile silence. When Elijah heard it, he buried his face in his cloak and went out to stand by the mouth of the cave where a voice spoke to him asking, "What are you doing here, Elijah?" (1 Kings 19:11–13)

The "terrible wind" is the rush of thoughts racing through our mind. We will let them pass and focus on the reading, because the angel that will lead us from ego-centered mind toward God-centered spirit cannot be found in the intellectual rush of ideas. The "earthquake" is the unleashing of emotions that often accompanies the settling of body and mind. These feelings can be captivating for the ego-centered mind, but they are a distraction. We need to stay focused on our reading and let the feelings pass of their own accord. The "fire" is the sense of energy that comes with the initial breakthrough of ego-centered mind into world-centered soul. This is the imagination lifting the ego out of its isolating box and into the larger reality. But this is not the end of the imaginative unfolding, only its prelude. After the fire, when body, mind, and emotions are still, we hear the "voice of fragile silence."

This voice, famously but incorrectly translated as the "still small voice" of God in the King James Bible, is "silent" in that it transcends words. The creative reading of our passage, our chosen angel myth, leads to silence. But this silence is not empty of meaning, for out of it comes the fundamental question of the angelic way, "What are you doing here?"

Here is another example of a possible reading, Hagar's first encounter with an angel recounted in Genesis. Rather than read it swiftly, we break up the passage into breathed clauses:

> The angel of YHVH found her by an oasis in the wilderness,
> the watering place on the road to Shur.
> And he said to her,
> "Hagar, servant of Sarai,
> where have you come from and where are you going?"
> "I am fleeing Sarai, my mistress."
> The angel of YHVH continued speaking, saying,
> "Return to your mistress, and surrender to her."
> Again the angel of YHVH spoke to her saying,
> "I will increase your descendants so greatly
> that they will be too numerable to count."
> And the angel of YHVH said to her,
> "You are pregnant and shall give birth to a son;
> you shall call him Ishmael,
> for YHVH has taken note of your suffering."
> (Genesis 16:7–11)

Read in this slow and distinct way the passage is more apt to yield something of interest to us. Perhaps it is the question "Where have you come from and where are you going?" that grabs us. Or perhaps the command to "return and surrender" speaks to our situation at the moment. Different passages will "choose us," meaning they will especially resonate with us depending on what is going on in our life at the time of the reading.

Once the passage has chosen us, it will come to greater and greater levels of clarity as we continue with the lectio divina practice. "Where have you come from?" could be a great existential question, or it might strike us as more prosaic. We might answer, "I come from God," or "I come from the universe," or "I am stardust become conscious." Or we might hear ourselves responding, "I have just come from a very stressful meeting at work, and I am worried that I am in danger of losing my job."

Following this last line and focusing on such a major concern, the second part of the question, "Where are you going?" may be very challenging. It may be that the thought of "trying to hold on" makes us more uncomfortable than the thought of "trying to let go." It may be that our answer to "Where are you going?" is an honest "I have no idea where I am going!"

The point is not to come up with some formal answer to the question—indeed in many cases the passage that chooses us is not a question at all—but simply to allow ourselves to feel connected to the passage. We need to take the text personally. And when we do so we enter into the second stage of lectio divina, *meditatio*.

Meditatio

Meditatio, meditation, is not the kind of meditative practice normally associated with Hinduism or Buddhism. In these traditions the aim of meditation is to release one's thoughts, but in meditatio as we are applying it here, the goal is to engage in imaginative thought.

As we enter into the deeper layers of the passage and myth we have chosen, we try to place ourselves imaginatively in it. We imagine ourselves like Elijah in the desert, or like Mary encountering an angel, or our meeting Amida Buddha or any of the other angelic beings or ascended humans we have read about, as well as the many others we have not.

We read the text again, and this time we let our imagination run loose. For example, we may imagine that we rather than Hagar are the protagonist in this story. We ask ourselves, "What am I running away from?" or "What is the wilderness I am running into?"

Now we are no longer just reading, but actively imagining. We should close our eyes after rereading the text and imagine the scene as vividly as we can. Let us not try and match the biblical landscape, but allow our own scene to arise. Hagar is in the desert, but we may find ourselves by an ocean or in a forest or on an empty street. What is the scene that we imagine? What does it mean to us? What does the angel with whom we are in contact look like and sound like?

We should not manage this stage of meditatio as if we were directing a play, but simply allow it to manifest as it will. We are an observer, but not a passive one. Perhaps the best notion of our role is that of a participant-observer: we are engaged in the myth unfolding yet we watch it unfold at the same time. Can we allow ourselves to be surprised by what we find, what we hear, and what we say? The story should unfold on its own.

This will take some practice. It may be difficult for the ego-centered mind to let go of control in this way. But the rewards are worth it. We are reaching beyond passive intellect to active intellect, intuition, and imagination. As mentioned, Aristotle understood passive intellect as the known, and active intellect as engaging with the as yet unknown. If we find ourselves responding to the unfolding myth with "Ah! I knew it!" we may very well not be engaging in imaginative thought at all, but only projecting the ego-centered mind's passive knowledge onto the text passage, making the discovery of something new next to impossible.

Meditatio should be surprising, perhaps at times challenging. It should shatter the *achad* of the ego, the sense of alienation and isolation that feeds both the ego-centered mind's illusion of itself as the whole and the suffering that accompanies this illusion. If we are quite comfortable with what we experience, chances are we are not yet practicing the lectio divina of the angelic way.

Returning to Hagar, or rather to us in Hagar's situation, the question the angel poses, "Where have you come from and where are you going?" is clearly addressed to us and us alone. And given our practical example that we might be coming from a business meeting that seems to threaten our job, the question "Where are you going?" takes on special importance.

We may not know where we are going. Fine. Let us allow the angel to inquire differently, "Where do you want to go?" or "Where might you go if you do lose your job?" The angel should be free to do so. Of course this is our myth, our imagination, but let us not write out a script for the encounter in advance. It needs to happen freely.

As we move through the meditatio stage of lectio divina there will be moments when we might be moved deeply or rocked by surprise. We should do our best to remain still and observe these moments, looking more deeply into them rather than being distracted by them. In this way we are imitating the prophet Elijah who waited through the distractions of wind, earthquake, and fire to hear the astonishingly fresh voice of God that arises out of the silence of the full self (mind, soul, and spirit) in meditatio. And when these moments happen we move on to stage three, *oratio*.

Oratio

Oratio, prayer, moves the lectio divina even deeper. We have found ourselves addressed by an angel or holy messenger. A question has been asked or a sign has been posted. We have been pointed in a certain direction of inquiry. Now the drama ceases, the myth is set aside, and we focus on the question or way-pointing alone. As with Elijah in the desert, all that remains now is the question "What am I doing here?" This question now becomes our prayer, our mantra. Nothing else matters but this, "What am I doing here?"

If we were to use the Hagar text the question might be "Where am I going?" or it may have morphed into "Where should I be going?" or "Where do I want to go?" or more simply, "Where is the way to my happiness or bliss?"

Whether it is a question or a sign, image, or something even more abstract, something will have arisen in the meditatio stage of lectio divina that will dominate our thinking and become the focus of oratio.

We know we are engaged fully in oratio when the question or sign just won't let go of us. It is what we need to know at this moment more than we need to know anything else. It is what the angel or other messenger from God wants to tell us. But before the angel can reveal the meaning of this sign or the answer to this question, *we* must become the sign or the question. No other thoughts can distract us. The myth is set aside, or more accurately it is simply forgotten. The reading is over. So strong has our imagination made our encounter with the angelic that we have almost forgotten that this is lectio divina. It feels deeply personal, and the question or sign is burning inside us.

Oratio is *not* a time for polite prayer, like "O God, if it be thy will, please bestow upon your humble servant insight . . ." We are wrestling with the question or sign in this stage of prayer with a real urgency, with a deep desire to reveal what is encapsulated in the prayer.

Perhaps this is where our angelic lectio divina differs from formal lectio divina. It may well be that the time we have set aside for this practice is over and we are still in the grips of oratio. Or it may be that we need more time to enter this third stage of the practice, but other obligations demand that we move on. The wonderful thing about our lectio divina is that it moves on with us.

Once the seed of the myth is planted, that is to say once we have actively imagined ourselves into a story, the story will accompany us as we go about the demands of our everyday life. The "prayer" that has emerged from the myth will rest in the back of our mind, pushing against the limits of ego-centered mind until, whether we are expecting it or not, new insight arises. Our practice sets the process in motion, and doing this regularly deepens our ability to move into oratio and be taken over by the prayer. It also deepens our capacity, without willful action on our part, to slip from stage three to stage four, from oratio to *comtemplatio*, where we will hear and ponder the angelic message.

Contemplatio

In the final stage of lectio divina, *contemplatio* or contemplation, our prayer yields some new insight or wisdom. And for it to do so we must learn to listen.

Listening is among the most intimate acts of love. Listening means being fully receptive to the other, whether that other is a person, an angel, or God. But the listening of contemplatio is not a willed action; it is a gift of grace. We cannot force ourselves to listen, we can only cease any active resistance to listening.

The truth is, however, that when the prayer has us fully enriched there is no need to worry about listening; it comes naturally from the intensity of the prayer. Our inquiry into why we are here (to take Elijah's story), or where we have come from and where we may be going (to draw from Hagar's story), or whatever it is the myth has birthed in us, is so powerful, so deep, so transforming that we cannot slip into an ego-centered response without a jarring sense of inauthenticity. We can no longer mistake the shrill voice of ego for the silent voice of God.

What arises in this stage of contemplatio is true because whatever it is, it does not serve the illusion of alienation but the healing of belonging. Whatever we hear in response to our prayer is true if it is in service to life lived in the greater, more inclusive levels of consciousness—I-Thou and I-I.

We cannot know in advance what we will be offered in contemplatio, nor should we think it will be the same every time we engage in lectio divina. In fact we can be certain that if the revelation is always the same it is either because we intentionally continue to listen to it, or because we are interfering with the process and simply hearing what the ego-centered mind wants to hear.

During formal lectio practice when we are sitting alone, contemplatio is just that—sitting. Even the active imagination falls silent here. Nothing is left: the myth, the active engagement in the myth, the questions and signs—all are gone. We are simply alone with the silence, and, when grace allows, with God's voice that is at the heart of silence.

Practicing Lectio Divina with Others

Originally lectio divina was designed for individual practice, but over time a practice for groups has developed, and we would be remiss if we didn't touch on this as well. While group practice is not a substitute for solitary practice, it may be an aid to it.

If we choose to explore lectio divina in a group setting, we should keep the group small, no more than eight to ten people. Someone from within the group takes on the role of facilitator, choosing the myth to be read and reading it aloud slowly twice, with a few minutes of silence separating each reading so that the words and images can sink into the imagination of the listeners. The first reading simply gets the group familiar with the passage, the myth; the second reading allows them to step into it. This is the first stage of the practice, lectio.

The facilitator then passes the text to another person (of the opposite sex if the group is mixed), who then reads the text slowly a third time. Having a different voice now frees the mind from stereotypes. With this third reading the second stage, meditatio, begins, and members are encouraged to actively and imaginatively place themselves in the myth, either alongside the myth's protagonist or in place of the protagonist. Silence again follows the reading, this time ten minutes, time enough to allow the active imagination to begin to engage with the myth and make it one's own.

It is in this silence that the question or sign emerges. Our imaginations begin to blend the myth with our current life situation. The myth unfolds in ways that leave the fixed reading behind.

A fourth reading of the text, again by the second reader, signals the shift from meditatio to oratio, from engaging with the myth to praying the myth. Again the reading is followed by ten minutes of silence in which the sign or question takes hold.

After those ten minutes a bell is sounded, signaling the final stage, contemplatio. Now we simply sit in silence and listen. Our minds are, to the best of our ability, free from myth, story, signs, and questions. The seeds have been planted and now we await the sprouts of insight. Contemplatio should last for ten minutes at the very least. Nothing may happen during this formal listening period, but we can expect a harvest in time, often at the least expected place or moment.

Three peals of the bell signal the end of contemplatio. The facilitator then invites participants to share their experiences, reminding all assembled to honor both the practice and their fellow participants by abstaining from cross talk, commentary, advice giving. The goal here is simply to share what one has heard with the others in the group.

When the time is up, or when no more words are forthcoming, the facilitator should thank the group for assembling and sharing, and remind everyone that our respect for one another and this process requires that we do not repeat what we have heard from others in the group to anybody outside the group.

• • •

This book opened with a question: Why do angels have wings? Let us end with the same question. Why do we imagine angels with wings? We do so because on a deep intuitive level we know that angels are messengers traveling from one dimension of consciousness to another: from ego-centered mind through world-centered soul to God-centered spirit, and back again. Angels are the human faculty of imagination flying beyond the limits of ego and the I-It level of consciousness where everything serves "me," to the I-Thou level where we serve one another, and to the I-I level where we realize that I and Thou are both part of a greater whole, the absolute unity we call God.

Angels are not separate from us, but aspects of us. Our myths reveal this time and again when they share tales of humans mistaking angels for humans, and humans becoming angels, and humans ascending to the realm of angels to dwell among them and to return to humankind with messages of hope and solace.

Angels are not figments of our imagination but the imagination itself. Angels are not external to us but internal. Angels do not rescue us, but symbolize our capacity to rescue ourselves from the trap of ego-centered isolation. Angels are not guardians protecting the ego, but guardians challenging the ego to open up to soul and spirit. Angels are symbolic of our capacity to move from mind to soul to spirit and back again, allowing each dimension to be enriched by the wisdom and insight of the others. Angels are not so much messengers from God, but guides pointing the way to God.

Angels have wings because angels are us, and we can fly.

Notes

New Testament quotations are from the New Revised Standard Version Bible: Catholic Edition, copyright 1989, 1993, Division of Christian Education of the National Council of the Churches of Christ in the United States of America. Used by permission. All rights reserved.

INTRODUCTION

1. Plato, *Phaedrus*, trans. Alexander Nehamas and Paul Woodruff. Indianapolis: Hackett Publishing Company, 1995, p. 33.
2. *Tao Te Ching: A New English Version*, trans. Stephen Mitchell. New York: Harper & Row, 1988, p. 1.
3. Peter L. Berger, *A Rumor of Angels: Modern Society and the Rediscovery of the Supernatural.* Garden City, NY: Anchor Books, 1970, p. 94.
4. William Blake, *The Marriage of Heaven and Hell*, ed. Sir Geoffrey Keynes. New York: Oxford University Press, 1975, p. xvi.
5. Joseph Campbell, *The Inner Reaches of Outer Space: Metaphor as Myth and as Religion.* Novato, CA: New World Library, 2002, p. 5.
6. Joseph Campbell, *The Hero's Journey: Joseph Campbell on His Life and Work.* New York: New World Library, 2003, p. 134.
7. Mark Meadows, "Campbell and the Perennial Philosophy: Social Sciences, Mysticism, and Myth," in Kenneth L. Golden, ed., *Uses of Comparative Mythology: Essays on the Work of Joseph Campbell.* New York: Garland Publishing, 1992, p. 253.
8. Joseph Campbell, *The Inner Reaches of Outer Space: Metaphor as Myth and as Religion.* Novato, CA: New World Library, 2002, pp. 27–28.
9. *Chandogya Upanisad*, Part 6, Chapter 8, Verse 7, in *The Upanisads*, trans. Valerie J. Roebuck. New York: Penguin, 2004, p. 176.

CHAPTER ONE

1. Harold Bloom, *Omens of the Millennium: The Gnosis of Angels, Dreams, and Resurrection.* New York: Riverhead Books, 1996, p. 55.
2. Harold Bloom, *Omens of the Millennium: The Gnosis of Angels, Dreams, and Resurrection.* New York: Riverhead Books, 1996, p. 55.
3. Edward Sell, *The Faith of Islam.* London: SPCK Press, 1920, p. 278.
4. *The Qur'an: A New Translation*, trans. M. A. S. Abdel Haleem. New York: Oxford University Press, 2004, p. 204.
5. *The Qur'an: A New Translation*, trans. M. A. S. Abdel Haleem. New York: Oxford University Press, 2004, p. 301.
6. *The Qur'an: A New Translation*, trans. M. A. S. Abdel Haleem. New York: Oxford University Press, 2004, p. 154.
7. *The Qur'an: A New Translation*, trans. M. A. S. Abdel Haleem. New York: Oxford University Press, 2004, p. 43.
8. *The Qur'an: A New Translation*, trans. M. A. S. Abdel Haleem. New York: Oxford University Press, 2004, p. 84.
9. *The Qur'an: A New Translation*, trans. M. A. S. Abdel Haleem. New York: Oxford University Press, 2004, p. 319.
10. Edward Sell, *The Faith of Islam.* London: SPCK Press, 1920, p. 201.

11. Barbara Daly Metcalf, *Perfecting Women: Maulana Ashraf 'Ali Thanawi's Bihishti Zewar*. Berkeley: University of California Press, 1992, p. 71.
12. *The Qur'an: A New Translation*, trans. M. A. S. Abdel Haleem. New York: Oxford University Press, 2004, p. 163.
13. Nathaniel Altman, *The Deva Handbook: How to Work with Nature's Subtle Energies*. Rochester, VT: Destiny Books, 1995, p. 4.
14. *The Rig Veda*, trans. Wendy Doniger. New York: Penguin, 2005, p. 25.
15. *The Rig Veda*, trans. Wendy Doniger. New York: Penguin, 2005, p. 36.
16. Jeanine Miller, *The Vision of Cosmic Order in the Vedas*. London: Routledge & Kegan Paul Books Ltd, 1985, p. 72.
17. *The Hymns of the RGVEDA*, trans. Ralph T. H. Griffith. Delhi: Motilal Banarsidass, 1986, p. 367.
18. *The Hymns of the RGVEDA*, trans. Ralph T. H. Griffith. Delhi: Motilal Banarsidass, 1986, p. 293.
19. *The Hymns of the RGVEDA*, trans. Ralph T. H. Griffith. Delhi: Motilal Banarsidass, 1986, p. 111.
20. Franklin Edgerton, ed., *The Beginnings of Indian Philosophy: Selections from the Rig Veda, Atharva Veda, Upanisads, and Mahabharata*. Cambridge, MA: Harvard University Press, 1965, p. 108.
21. Jeanine Miller, "The Shining Ones of the Vedas," in Maria Parisen, comp., *Angels and Mortals: Their Co-Creative Power*. Wheaton, IL: Quest Books, 1990, p. 87.
22. *The Long Discourses of the Buddha: A Translation of the Digha Nikaya*, trans. Maurice Walshe. Boston: Wisdom Publications, 1995, electronic version Columbia University, unpaginated (www.columbia.edu/itc/religion/f2001/edit/docs/aggannasutta.pdf).

CHAPTER TWO
1. *The Zohar*, Prizker Edition, Vol. II, trans. Daniel C. Matt. Stanford, CA: Stanford University Press, 2004, p. 257.
2. Raphael Ben Zion, trans., *An Anthology of Jewish Mysticism*. New York: Judaica Press, 1981, p. 161.
3. Raphael Ben Zion, trans., *An Anthology of Jewish Mysticism*. New York: Judaica Press, 1981, p. 162.
4. Raphael Ben Zion, trans., *An Anthology of Jewish Mysticism*. New York: Judaica Press, 1981, p. 162.
5. *Midrash Rabbah: Genesis Rabbah*, Vol. II, trans. H. Freedman. New York: Soncino Press, 1983, p. 626.
6. *Midrash Rabbah: Genesis Rabbah*, Vol. II, trans. H. Freedman. New York: Soncino Press, 1983, p. 626.
7. Louis Ginzberg, *The Legends of the Jews*. Philadelphia: Jewish Publication Society, 1956, p. 310, retold by author.
8. Thomas Patrick Hughes, *A Dictionary of Islam*. London: Laurier Books, Ltd, 1996, p. 620.
9. Thomas Patrick Hughes, *A Dictionary of Islam*. London: Laurier Books, Ltd, 1996, p. 620.

CHAPTER THREE
1. Louis Ginzberg, *The Legends of the Jews*. Philadelphia: Jewish Publication Society, 1956, p. 109, retold by author.
2. Louis Ginzberg, *The Legends of the Jews*. Philadelphia: Jewish Publication Society, 1956, pp. 110–111, retold by author.
3. *Midrash Rabbah: Genesis Rabbah*, Vol. II, trans. H. Freedman. New York: Soncino Press, 1983, p. 434.
4. Louis Ginzberg, *The Legends of the Jews*. Philadelphia: Jewish Publication Society, 1956, pp. 116–117, retold by author.
5. Louis Ginzberg, *The Legends of the Jews*. Philadelphia: Jewish Publication Society, 1956, p. 118, retold by author.

6. Louis Ginzberg, *The Legends of the Jews*. Philadelphia: Jewish Publication Society, 1956, p. 123, retold by author.

7. *Midrash Rabbah: Genesis Rabbah*, Vol. II, trans. H. Freedman. New York: Soncino Press, 1983, p. 710, retold by author.

8. Louis Ginzberg, *The Legends of the Jews*. Philadelphia: Jewish Publication Society, 1956, p. 133, retold by author.

CHAPTER FOUR

1. *Midrash Rabbah: Genesis Rabbah*, Vol. I, trans. H. Freedman. New York: Soncino Press, 1983, p. 58, retold by author.

2. Louis Ginzberg, *The Legends of the Jews*. Philadelphia: Jewish Publication Society, 1956, p. 28, retold by author.

3. *Midrash Rabbah: Genesis Rabbah*, Vol. I, trans. H. Freedman. New York: Soncino Press, 1983, p. 74, retold by author.

4. Augustine, *Eight Questions*, cited in Gustav Davidson, *A Dictionary of Angels: Including the Fallen Angels*. New York: Free Press, 1967, p. xii.

5. Ibn Ishaq, *The Life of Muhammad*, trans. Alfred Guillaume. Oxford: Oxford University Press, 2004, p. 107.

6. *The Qur'an: A New Translation*, trans. M. A. S. Abdel Haleem. New York: Oxford University Press, 2004, p. 192.

7. James H. Charlesworth, ed., *The Old Testament Pseudepigrapha*, Vol. I. Garden City, NY: Doubleday, 1990, p. 529.

8. James H. Charlesworth, ed., *The Old Testament Pseudepigrapha*, Vol. I. Garden City, NY: Doubleday, 1990, p. 545.

9. James H. Charlesworth, ed., *The Old Testament Pseudepigrapha*, Vol. I. Garden City, NY: Doubleday, 1990, p. 541.

CHAPTER FIVE

1. Harold Bloom, *Fallen Angels*. New Haven, CT: Yale University Press, 2007, p. 11.

2. Charles F. Horne, trans., *The Sacred Books and Early Literature of the East, Vol. VII: Ancient Persia*. Whitefish, MT: Kessinger Publishing Company, 1997, p. 195.

3. Elaine Pagels, *The Origin of Satan: How Christians Demonized Jews, Pagans, and Heretics*. New York: Random House, 1995, pp. 39–40.

4. Louis Ginzberg, *The Legends of the Jews*. Philadelphia: Jewish Publication Society, 1956, p. 127, retold by author.

5. Louis Ginzberg, *The Legends of the Jews*. Philadelphia: Jewish Publication Society, 1956, p. 128, retold by author.

6. Louis Ginzberg, *The Legends of the Jews*. Philadelphia: Jewish Publication Society, 1956, p. 131, retold by author.

7. Morris B. Margolies, *A Gathering of Angels: Angels in Jewish Life and Literature*. New York: Ballantine, 1994, p. 109.

8. James H. Charlesworth, ed., *The Old Testament Pseudepigrapha*, Vol. II. Garden City, NY: Doubleday, 1990, p. 157.

9. Elaine Pagels, *The Origin of Satan: How Christians Demonized Jews, Pagans, and Heretics*. New York: Random House, 1995, p. 49.

10. Bhikkhu Naanamoli, *The Life of the Buddha: According to the Pali Canon*. Kandy: Buddhist Publication Society, 1972, p. 19.

11. *Buddha's Teachings—Being the Sutta Nipata or Discourse Collection*, trans. Lord Chalmers. Cambridge, MA: Harvard Oriental Series, 1932, p. 105.
12. *Buddha's Teachings—Being the Sutta Nipata or Discourse Collection*, trans. Lord Chalmers. Cambridge, MA: Harvard Oriental Series, 1932, p. 105.
13. Bernard J. Bamberger, *Fallen Angels*. New York: Jewish Publication Society, 1952, p. 76.
14. Bernard J. Bamberger, *Fallen Angels*. New York: Jewish Publication Society, 1952, pp. 81–82.
15. Bernard J. Bamberger, *Fallen Angels*. New York: Jewish Publication Society, 1952, p. 83.
16. *Al-Qur'an: A Contemporary Translation*, trans. Ahmed Ali. Princeton, NJ: Princeton University Press, 2001, p. 15.
17. Abu Jafar Muhammad ibn Jarir al-Tabari, cited in Leo Jung, *Fallen Angels in Jewish, Christian and Mohammedan Literature*. London: University of London, 1926, p. 60.

CHAPTER SIX

1. Erik Stave, "Aeshma (Asmodeus, Ashmedai)," www.jewishencyclopedia.com.
2. Louis Ginzberg, *The Legends of the Jews*. Philadelphia: Jewish Publication Society, 1956, pp. 85–86, retold by author.
3. *Ma'aseh Book: Book of Jewish Tales and Legends*, Vol. I, trans. Moses Gaster. Philadelphia: Jewish Publication Society, 1934, p. 30, retold by author.
4. Louis Ginzberg, *The Legends of the Jews*. Philadelphia: Jewish Publication Society, 1956, pp. 499–502, retold by author.
5. *Al-Qur'an: A Contemporary Translation*, trans. Ahmed Ali. Princeton, NJ: Princeton University Press, 2001, p. 353.
6. Nagendra Kumar Singh, *Encyclopaedia of Hinduism*. New Delhi: Crescent, 2007, p. 1795, retold by author.

CHAPTER SEVEN

1. While we are dealing with myth, there is an actual *Sefer Raziel* that is a thirteenth-century Jewish mystical text originating among the Franco-German Jewish Pietists called the *Chassidei Ashkenaz* (the Pious Ones of *Ashkenaz*, the Hebrew word referring to the Rhineland and northern France). Most scholars believe the texts of the book were compiled and edited by Eleazer of Worms (c. 1160–1230), who was a major rabbi, mystic, and author. The *Sefer Raziel* is divided into five books filled with a detailed angelology, magical spells, and methods for writing healing amulets.
2. Gustav Davidson, *A Dictionary of Angels: Including the Fallen Angels*. New York: Free Press, 1967, p. 242.
3. Louis Ginzberg, *The Legends of the Jews*. Philadelphia: Jewish Publication Society, 1956, pp. 86–87, retold by author.
4. Louis Ginzberg, *The Legends of the Jews*. Philadelphia: Jewish Publication Society, 1956, p. 64, retold by author.
5. *Zohar Hadash, Terumah*, 42d, cited in Isaiah Tishby, *The Wisdom of the Zohar: An Anthology of Texts*, Vol. II, London: Oxford University Press, 1991, p. 627, retold by author.
6. Isaiah Tishby, *The Wisdom of the Zohar: An Anthology of Texts*, Vol. II, London: Oxford University Press, 1991, p. 627.
7. *Zohar* 1, 37b, 56b.
8. Elliot R. Wolfson, *Through a Speculum that Shines: Vision and Imagination in Medieval Jewish Mysticism*. Princeton, NJ: Princeton University Press, 1994, p. 224.
9. Gustav Davidson, *A Dictionary of Angels: Including the Fallen Angels*. New York: Free Press, 1967, p. 192.

10. Isaiah Tishby, *The Wisdom of the Zohar: An Anthology of Texts*, Vol. II, London: Oxford University Press, 1991, p. 631.
11. Harold Bloom, *Omens of the Millennium: The Gnosis of Angels, Dreams, and Resurrection*. New York: Riverhead Books, 1996, p. 207.
12. Hayim Nahman Bialik and Yeshoshua Hana Ravnitzky, eds., *The Book of Legends/Sefer Ha-Aggadah: Legends from the Talmud and Midrash*. New York: Schocken, 1992, p. 473.
13. Ms. Jerusalem, NUL 80 147, fols. 96b–97a, cited in Moshe Idel, *Ascensions on High in Jewish Mysticism: Pillars, Lines, Ladders*. New York: Central European University Press, 2005, pp. 55–56.
14. Howard Schwartz, *Tree of Souls: The Mythology of Judaism*. Oxford: Oxford University Press, 2004, p. 176, retold by author.
15. Pius XII, Munificentissimus Deus, in *Selected Documents of Pope Pius XII*. Washington, D.C.: National Catholic Welfare Conference, 1950, pp. 38, 40, 44–45, 47.
16. Peter M. J. Stravinskas, ed., *The Catholic Answer Book of Mary*. Huntington, IN: Our Sunday Visitor, 2000, p. 60.
17. Peter M. J. Stravinskas, ed., *The Catholic Answer Book of Mary*. Huntington, IN: Our Sunday Visitor, 2000, pp. 60–61.
18. Peter M. J. Stravinskas, ed., *The Catholic Answer Book of Mary*. Huntington, IN: Our Sunday Visitor, 2000, pp. 61–62.
19. Jenny Schroedel and John Schroedel, *The Everything Mary Book: The Life and Legacy of the Blessed Mother*. Avon, MA: Adams Media, 2006, p. 150.
20. *The Little Flowers of St. Francis*, trans. Roger Hudleston. Whitefish, MT: Kessinger Publishing, 2003, p. 174.
21. *Al-Qur'an: A Contemporary Translation*, trans. Ahmed Ali. Princeton, NJ: Princeton University Press, 2001, p. 240.
22. *Sahih Bukhari* Book 9, Chapter 93: 608. *Sahih Bukhari*, trans. M. Muhsin Khan. Los Angeles: University of Southern California, electronic text, unpaginated (www.usc.edu/schools/college/crcc/engagement/resources/texts/muslim/hadith/bukhari/).
23. Marie-Rose Seguy, *The Miraculous Journey of Mahomet*. New York: George Braziller, 1977, p. 14.
24. *Larger Sutra of Immeasurable Life*, cited in Donald S. Lopez, Jr., ed., *Buddhist Scriptures*. New York: Penguin, 2004, p. 384.
25. Alfred Bloom, ed., *The Essential Shinran: A Buddhist Path of True Entrusting*. Bloomington, IN: World Wisdom, 2007, p. 133.
26. Teitetsu Unno, *River of Fire, River of Water: An Introduction to the Pure Land Tradition of Shin Buddhism*. New York: Doubleday, 1998, p. 181.
27. Teitetsu Unno, *River of Fire, River of Water: An Introduction to the Pure Land Tradition of Shin Buddhism*. New York: Doubleday, 1998, pp. 181–182.

CHAPTER EIGHT

1. Joseph Campbell, *Myths of Light: Eastern Metaphors of the Eternal*. Novato, CA: New World Library, 2003, p. xvii.
2. Joseph Campbell, with Bill Moyers, *The Power of Myth*. New York: Broadway Books, 1988, p. 163.
3. Joseph Campbell, with Bill Moyers, *The Power of Myth*. New York: Broadway Books, 1988, p. 163.
4. Hirsch Loeb Gordon, *The Maggid of Caro: The Mystic Life of the Eminent Codifier Joseph Caro as Revealed in His Secret Diary*. New York: Pardes Publishing, 1949, p. 253.
5. Hirsch Loeb Gordon, *The Maggid of Caro: The Mystic Life of the Eminent Codifier Joseph Caro as Revealed in His Secret Diary*. New York: Pardes Publishing, 1949, pp. 253–54.

Bibliography

Abdul-Rauf, Muhammad, *Islam Creed and Worship*. Washington, D.C.: Islamic Center, 1974.

Adler, Gerhard, *The Living Symbol: A Case Study in the Process of Individuation*. New York: Pantheon Books, 1961.

Adler, Mortimer J., *The Angels and Us*. New York: Macmillan Publishing Company, 1982.

Alcott, A. Bronson, *How Like an Angel Came I Down: Conversations with Children on the Gospels*. Hudson, NY: Lindisfarne Press, 1991.

Altman, Nathaniel, *The Deva Handbook: How to Work with Nature's Subtle Energies*. Rochester, VT: Destiny Books, 1995.

Babb, Lawrence A., *The Divine Hierarchy: Popular Hinduism in Central India*. New York: Columbia University Press, 1975.

Baljon, J. M. S., trans., *A Mystical Interpretation of Prophetic Tales by an Indian Muslim: Shah Wali Alla's Tawil al-Ahadith*. Leiden: E. J. Brill, 1973.

Bamberger, Bernard J., *Fallen Angels*. New York: Jewish Publication Society, 1952.

Barnstone, Willis, ed., *The Other Bible*. San Francisco: HarperSanFrancisco, 2005.

Bennet, E. A., *What Jung Really Said*. New York: Schocken Books, 1966.

Ben Zion, Raphael, trans., *An Anthology of Jewish Mysticism*. New York: Judaica Press, 1981.

Berger, Peter L., *A Rumor of Angels: Modern Society and the Rediscovery of the Supernatural*. Garden City, NY: Anchor Books, 1970.

Berger, Peter L., ed., *The Other Side of God: A Polarity in World Religions*. New York: Anchor Press, 1981.

Bharati, Agehananda, ed., *The Realm of the Extra-Human: Agents and Audiences*. New York: Mouton, 1976.

Bhikkhu Naanamoli, *The Life of the Buddha: According to the Pali Canon*. Kandy: Buddhist Publication Society, 1972.

Bialik, Hayim Nahman, and Yeshoshua Hana Ravnitzky, eds., *The Book of Legends/Sefer Ha-Aggadah: Legends from the Talmud and Midrash*. New York: Schocken, 1992.

Blake, William, *The Marriage of Heaven and Hell*, ed. Sir Geoffrey Keynes. New York: Oxford University Press, 1975.

Bloom, Alfred, ed., *The Essential Shinran: A Buddhist Path of True Entrusting*. Bloomington, IN: World Wisdom, 2007.

Bloom, Harold, *Omens of the Millennium: The Gnosis of Angels, Dreams, and Resurrection*. New York: Riverhead Books, 1996.

Bloom, Harold, *Fallen Angels*. New Haven, CT: Yale University Press, 2007.

Boyce, Mary, *History of Zoroastrianism*, Vol. I. Leiden: Brill, 1996.

Boyce, Mary, *History of Zoroastrianism*, Vol. II. Leiden: Brill, 1997.

Boyce, Mary, "Ahura Mazda," in *Encyclopaedia Iranica*, Vol. I. New York: Mazda Publishers, 2002.

Boyce, Mary, "Amesha Spenta," in *Encyclopaedia Iranica*, Vol. I. New York: Mazda Publishers, 2002.

Briggs, Constance Victoria, *The Encyclopedia of Angels: An A-to-Z Guide with Nearly 4,000 Entries*. New York: Plume, 1997.

Brisson, Luc, and Catherine Tihanyi, *How Philosophers Saved Myths: Allegorical Interpretation and Classical Mythology*. Chicago: University of Chicago Press, 2004.

Browman, David L., and Ronald A. Schwarz, eds., *Spirits, Shamans, and Stars: Perspectives from South America*. New York: Mouton, 1979.

Buddha's Teachings—Being the Sutta Nipata or Discourse Collection, trans. Lord Chalmers. Cambridge, MA: Harvard Oriental Series, 1932.

Catholic Encyclopedia. New York: Robert Appleton Company, 1907.

Campbell, Joseph, *The Hero With A Thousand Faces.* Princeton, NJ: Princeton University Press, 1949.

Campbell, Joseph, with Bill Moyers, *The Power of Myth.* New York: Broadway Books, 1988.

Campbell, Joseph, *The Inner Reaches of Outer Space: Metaphor as Myth and as Religion.* Novato, CA: New World Library, 2002.

Campbell, Joseph, *Myths of Light: Eastern Metaphors of the Eternal.* Novato, CA: New World Library, 2003.

Campbell, Joseph, *The Hero's Journey: Joseph Campbell on His Life and Work.* New York: New World Library, 2003.

Campbell, Joseph, *Pathways to Bliss: Mythology and Personal Transformation.* Novato, CA: New World Library, 2004.

Charlesworth, James H., ed., *The Old Testament Pseudepigrapha,* Vol. I. Garden City, NY: Doubleday, 1990.

Charlesworth, James H., ed., *The Old Testament Pseudepigrapha,* Vol. II. Garden City, NY: Doubleday, 1990.

Cheetham, Tom, *The World Turned Inside Out: Henry Corbin and Islamic Mysticism.* Woodstock, CT: Spring Journal Books, 2003.

Cheetham, Tom, *Green Man, Earth Angel: The Prophetic Tradition and the Battle for the Soul of the World.* New York: SUNY Press, 2005.

Cooper, David A., *Invoking Angels: For Blessings, Protection, and Healing.* Boulder, CO: Sounds True, 2006.

Corbin, Henry, ed., *Spiritual Body and Celestial Earth: From Mazdean Iran to Shi'ite Iran.* Princeton, NJ: Princeton University Press, 1977.

Cruz, Joan Carroll, *Angels and Devils.* Rockford, IL: Tan Books & Publishers, 1999.

Dan, Joseph, *Kabbalah: A Very Short Introduction.* Oxford: Oxford University Press, 2006.

Danielou, Jean, *The Angels and Their Mission: According to the Fathers of the Church.* Dublin: Four Courts Press, 1953.

Davidson, Gustav, *A Dictionary of Angels: Including the Fallen Angels.* New York: Free Press, 1967.

Duchesne-Guillemin, Jacques, "Ahriman," in *Encyclopaedia Iranica,* Vol. I. New York: Mazda Publishers, 2002.

Durckheim, Karlfried Graf, *The Way of Transformation: Daily Life as Spiritual Exercise.* London: Allen & Unwin, 1988.

Edgerton, Franklin, ed., *The Beginnings of Indian Philosophy: Selections from the Rig Veda, Atharva Veda, Upanisads, and Mahabharata.* Cambridge, MA: Harvard University Press, 1965.

Eliade, Mircea, *Shamanism: Archaic Techniques of Ecstasy.* New York: Bollingen Foundation, 1964.

Ford-Grabowsky, Mary, *Spiritual Writings on Mary: Annotated and Explained.* Woodstock, VT: Skylight Paths, 2005.

Fox, Matthew, and Rupert Sheldrake, *The Physics of Angels: Exploring the Realm Where Science and Spirit Meet.* San Francisco: HarperSanFrancisco, 1996.

Frankfort, Henri, *Before Philosophy: The Intellectual Adventure of Ancient Man.* Baltimore: Penguin Books, 1949.

Fromm, Erich, *On Being Human.* New York: Continuum, 1994.

Gambero, Luigi, *Mary in the Middle Ages: The Blessed Virgin Mary in the Thought of Medieval Latin Theologians.* San Francisco: Ignatius Press, 2000.

Gerth, Hans, and C. Wright Mills, eds., *From Max Weber: Essays in Sociology.* New York: Oxford University Press, 1946.

Ginzberg, Louis, *The Legends of the Jews.* Philadelphia: Jewish Publication Society, 1956.

Gokey, Francis X., *The Terminology for the Devil and Evil Spirits in the Apostolic Fathers*. Washington, D.C.: Catholic University of America Press, 1961.

Golden, Kenneth L., ed., *Uses of Comparative Mythology: Essays on the Work of Joseph Campbell*. New York: Garland Publishing, 1992.

Gordon, Hirsch Loeb, *The Maggid of Caro: The Mystic Life of the Eminent Codifier Joseph Caro as Revealed in His Secret Diary*. New York: Pardes Publishing, 1949.

Green, Arthur, "Hasidism: Discovery and Retreat," in Peter L. Berger, ed., *The Other Side of God: A Polarity in World Religions*. New York: Anchor Press, 1981.

Harner, Michael, *The Way of the Shaman: A Guide to Power and Healing*. San Francisco: Harper & Row, 1980.

Haynes, Stephen R., *Reluctant Witnesses: Jews and the Christian Imagination*. Louisville, KY: Westminster John Knox Press, 1995.

Heisig, James W., *Imago Dei: A Study of C. G. Jung's Psychology of Religion*. Lewisburg, PA: Bucknell University Press, 1979.

Hillman, James, *Archetypal Psychology*. Dallas: Spring Publications, 1988.

Holland, Barron, *Popular Hinduism and Hindu Mythology: An Annotated Bibliography*. Westport, CT: Greenwood Press, 1979.

Hopcke, R. H., *A Guided Tour of the Collected Works of C. G. Jung*. Boston: Shambhala, 1989.

Horne, Charles F., trans., *The Sacred Books and Early Literature of the East, Vol. VII: Ancient Persia*. Whitefish, MT: Kessinger Publishing Company, 1997.

Hughes, Thomas Patrick, *A Dictionary of Islam*. London: Laurier Books, Ltd, 1996.

The Hymns of the RGVEDA, trans. Ralph T. H. Griffith. Delhi: Motilal Banarsidass, 1986.

Ibn Ishaq, *The Life of Muhammad*, trans. Alfred Guillaume. Oxford: Oxford University Press, 2004.

Idel, Moshe, *Ascensions on High in Jewish Mysticism: Pillars, Lines, Ladders*. New York: Central European University Press, 2005.

Isaacs, Ronald H., *Ascending Jacob's Ladder: Jewish Views of Angels, Demons, and Evil Spirits*. Northvale, NJ: Jason Aronson, 1998.

Jaffe, Aniela, *The Myth of Meaning*. New York: G. P. Putnam's Sons, 1971.

Jaynes, Julian, *The Origin of Consciousness in the Breakdown of the Bicameral Mind*. New York: Houghton Mifflin Company, 2000.

Johnson, Robert A., *Inner Work: Using Dreams and Active Imagination for Personal Growth*. San Francisco: Harper, 1989.

Johnson, Robert A., *Owning Your Own Shadow: Understanding the Dark Side of the Psyche*. San Francisco: HarperSanFrancisco, 1991.

Jones, Lindsay, ed., *Encyclopedia of Religion*. New York: Thomson Gale, 2005.

Jung, Carl G., *Modern Man in Search of a Soul*. New York: Harcourt, Brace and Company, 1933.

Jung, Leo, *Fallen Angels in Jewish, Christian and Mohammedan Literature*. London: University of London, 1926.

Kalweit, Holger, *Shamans, Healers, and Medicine Men*. Boston: Shambhala, 1992.

Keck, David, *Angels and Angelology in the Middle Ages*. Oxford: Oxford University Press, 1998.

Kugel, James L., *The Ladder of Jacob: Ancient Interpretations of the Biblical Story of Jacob and His Children*. Princeton, NJ: Princeton University Press, 2006.

Laine, Daniel, *African Gods: Contemporary Rituals and Beliefs*. London: Thames & Hudson, 2007.

The Little Flowers of St. Francis, trans. Roger Hudleston. Whitefish, MT: Kessinger Publishing, 2003.

The Long Discourses of the Buddha: A Translation of the Digha Nikaya, trans. Maurice Walshe. Boston: Wisdom Publications, 1995.

ᴄᴧ Bibliography ᴧᴐ

Lopez, Donald S., Jr., ed., *Buddhist Scriptures*. New York: Penguin, 2004.

Ma'aseh Book: Book of Jewish Tales and Legends, Vol. I, trans. Moses Gaster. Philadelphia: Jewish Publication Society, 1934.

Maimonides, Moses, *Guide for the Perplexed*, trans. Michael Friedlander. New York: Barnes & Noble, 2004.

Maneck, Susan Stiles, *The Death of Ahriman: Culture, Identity and Theological Change Among the Parsis of India*. Bombay: K. R. Cama Oriental Institute, 1997.

Margolies, Morris B., *A Gathering of Angels: Angels in Jewish Life and Literature*. New York: Ballantine, 1994.

Matt, Daniel C., *God & the Big Bang: Discovering Harmony Between Science & Spirituality*. Woodstock, VT: Jewish Lights, 1996.

McConkie, Oscar Walter, Jr., *Angels*. Salt Lake City: Deseret Book Company, 1975.

Meadows, Mark, "Campbell and the Perennial Philosophy: Social Sciences, Mysticism, and Myth," in Kenneth L. Golden, ed., *Uses of Comparative Mythology: Essays on the Work of Joseph Campbell*. New York: Garland Publishing, 1992.

Metcalf, Barbara Daly, *Perfecting Women: Maulana Ashraf 'Ali Thanawi's Bihishti Zewar*. Berkeley: University of California Press, 1992.

Midrash Rabbah, trans. H. Freedman. New York: Soncino Press, 1983.

Miller, Jeanine, *The Vision of Cosmic Order in the Vedas*. London: Routledge & Kegan Paul Books Ltd, 1985.

Miller, Jeanine, "The Shining Ones of the Vedas," in Maria Parisen, comp., *Angels and Mortals: Their Co-Creative Power*. Wheaton, IL: Quest Books, 1990, p. 87.

Oliver, Evelyn Dorothy, and James R. Lewis, *Angels A to Z*. New York: Visible Ink, 1996.

Ott, Ludwig, *Fundamentals of Catholic Dogma*. New York: Tan Books and Publishers Inc., 1960.

Ouaknin, Marc-Alain, *Mysteries of the Kabbalah*. New York: Abbeville Press, 2000.

Pagels, Elaine, *The Origin of Satan: How Christians Demonized Jews, Pagans, and Heretics*. New York: Random House, 1995.

Parisen, Maria, comp., *Angels and Mortals: Their Co-Creative Power*. Wheaton, IL: Quest Books, 1990.

Pius XII, Munificentissimus Deus, in *Selected Documents of Pope Pius XII*. Washington, D.C.: National Catholic Welfare Conference, 1950.

Plato, *Phaedrus*, trans. Alexander Nehamas and Paul Woodruff. Indianapolis: Hackett Publishing Company, 1995.

Al-Qur'an: A Contemporary Translation, trans. Ahmed Ali. Princeton, NJ: Princeton University Press, 2001.

The Qur'an: A New Translation, trans. M. A. S. Abdel Haleem. New York: Oxford University Press, 2004.

Razi, Najm al-Din, *The Path of God's Bondsmen from Origin to Return*, trans. Hamid Algar. Delmar, NY: Caravan Books, 1982.

Reines, Alvin J., *Maimonides and Abrabanel on Prophecy*. Cincinnati: Hebrew Union College Press, 1970.

The Rig Veda, trans. Wendy Doniger. New York: Penguin, 2005.

Rogers, Spencer L., *The Shaman: His Symbols and His Healing Power*. Springfield, IL: Charles C. Thomas, 1982.

Roth, Leon, *Spinoza, Descartes & Maimonides*. New York: Russell & Russell, 1963.

Sahih Bukhari, trans. M. Muhsin Khan. Los Angeles: University of Southern California, electronic text (www.usc.edu/schools/college/crcc/engagement/resources/texts/muslim/hadith/bukhari/).

Sardello, Robert, ed., *The Angels*. New York: Continuum, 1995.

Schimmel, Annemarie, *Mystical Dimensions of Islam*. Chapel Hill, NC: University of North Carolina Press, 1975.

Schipflinger, Thomas, *Sophia-Maria: A Holistic Vision of Creation*. York Beach, ME: Samuel Weiser, 1998.

Scholem, Gershom, *Major Trends in Jewish Mysticism*. New York: Schocken, 1965.

Schroedel, Jenny, and John Schroedel: *The Everything Mary Book: The Life and Legacy of the Blessed Mother*. Avon, MA: Adams Media, 2006.

Schwartz, Howard, *Tree of Souls: The Mythology of Judaism*. Oxford: Oxford University Press, 2004.

Seguy, Marie-Rose, *The Miraculous Journey of Mahomet*. New York: George Braziller, 1977.

Sell, Edward, *The Faith of Islam*. London: SPCK Press, 1920.

Sepher Rezial Hemelach: The Book of the Angel Rezial, trans. Steve Savedow. New York: Red Wheel/Weiser, 2000.

Singer, June, *Boundaries of the Soul: The Practice of Jung's Psychology*. New York: Doubleday & Company, 1972.

Singh, Nagendra Kumar, *Encyclopaedia of Hinduism*. New Delhi: Crescent, 2007.

Steinsaltz, Adin, *The Thirteen Petalled Rose: A Discourse on the Essence of Jewish Existence and Belief*. New York: Basic Books, 2006.

Stravinskas, Peter M. J., ed., *The Catholic Answer Book of Mary*. Huntington, IN: Our Sunday Visitor, 2000.

Suzuki, D. T., *Buddha of Infinite Light: The Teachings of Shin Buddhism, the Japanese Way of Wisdom and Compassion*. Boston: Shambhala, 1998.

Tao Te Ching: A New English Version, trans. Stephen Mitchell. New York: Harper & Row, 1988.

Tishby, Isaiah, *The Wisdom of the Zohar: An Anthology of Texts*. London: Oxford University Press, 1991.

Trachtenberg, Joshua, *Jewish Magic and Superstition: A Study in Folk Religion*. New York: Atheneum, 1982.

von Rad, Gerhard, *Old Testament Theology, Vol. I: The Theology of Israel's Historical Traditions*. New York: Harper and Row, 1962.

Unno, Teitetsu, *River of Fire, River of Water: An Introduction to the Pure Land Tradition of Shin Buddhism*. New York: Doubleday, 1998.

The Upanisads, trans. Valerie J. Roebuck. New York: Penguin, 2004.

Walsh, Roger, *World of Shamanism: New Views of an Ancient Tradition*. Woodbury, MN: Llewellyn Publications, 2007.

Williams, James G., "Origin of Satan," in *Theology Today*, October 1996.

Wilson, Peter Lamborn, *Angels: Messengers of the Gods*. New York: Pantheon, 1980.

Wink, Walter, *The Human Being: Jesus and the Enigma of the Son of the Man*. Minneapolis: Fortress Press, 2002.

Wolfson, Elliot R., *Through a Speculum that Shines: Vision and Imagination in Medieval Jewish Mysticism*. Princeton, NJ: Princeton University Press, 1994.

Wright, Vinita Hampton, *A Catalogue of Angels: The Heavenly, the Fallen, and the Holy Ones Among Us*. Brewster, MA: Paraclete Press, 2006.

Zarruq, Ahmad, *The Principles of Sufism*. Bristol, England: Amal Press, 2008.

The Zohar, Prizker Edition, Vol. II, trans. Daniel C. Matt. Stanford, CA: Stanford University Press, 2004.

Index